I0080068

The Valley of the Eight

Other books by Matt Bialer

POETRY

Radius (Les Editiones du Zaporogue) 2012
Already Here (Black Coffee Press 2012
Ark (Black Coffee Press) 2012
Black Powder (Black Coffee Press) 2013
Bridge (Leaky Boot Press) 2013
Tell Them What I Saw (PS Publishing) 2014
Ascent (JournalStone) 2014
He Walks on all Fours (Dynatox Ministtries) 2015
Kings of Men (Dynatox Ministries) 2015
Wing of Light (Les Editiones du Zaporogue) 2015
Frequencies (Leaky Boot Press) 2015
Formation (Weirdo Magnet) 2016
Distant Shores (Villipede) 2016
Wonder Weavers (JournalStone) 2016

PHOTOGRAPHY

More Than You Know (Les Edtiones du Zaporogue) 2011
A Moment's Notice (Les Editiones du Zaporogue) 2016

PAINTIING

Shadowbrook (Les Editiones du Zaporogue)) 2012

The Valley of the Eight

an epic poem

Matt Bialer

LEAKY BOOT PRESS

The Valley of the Eight
by Matt Bialer

First published in 2017 by
Leaky Boot Press
http://www.leakyboot.com

Copyright © 2017 Matt Bialer
All rights reserved

No part of this book may be reproduced or
transmitted in any form or by any means, elec-
tronic, mechanical, photocopying, recording, or
otherwise, without prior written permission of
the author.

ISBN: 978-1-909849-51-8

The Valley
of the Eight

Here we are
In the Valley of the Eight

The Valley of the Eight

When they find out
We are here

For Nuhun Gemisi

Nuhun Gemesi

Noah's Ark

They point to
Mt. Ararat

13 miles away

Which rises
Into the mist

Rises into the mist

And at the end of seven days
In the six hundredth year

Of the life of Noah

The waters of the Flood
Were upon the Earth

And all the fountains
Of the deep

Were broken up

And the windows of heaven
Were opened

And the rain was upon
The Earth forty days

And forty nights

The windows of heaven
Were opened

Here we are
In the Valley of the Eight

Noah and Naameh
His 3 sons
And their wives

The Valley of the Eight

When they find out
We are here

For Nuhun Gemisi

Nuhn Gemisi

They point to
Mt. Ararat

Which rises
Into the mist

Rises into the mist

And the windows of heaven
Were opened

Little village
In Turkey

Now called Arzep

Also called

Sagliksuyu
Or Sa Lik Suxu

Acid water in Turkish

We are shown
These strange large stones

Huge headstones
That look like anchors

Have been found

They have
Or had

Holes on top

Some are still intact
Still see the holes

Here in this village
And throughout hills

Surrounding the region

Thirteen such stones
Have been found

Thirteen such stones

2 even 3 meters

Holes in the stones
Are special

Slope inwards

Fit to tie a rope

So knot
Slides into the hole

Stays put

Create a drag
In the water

If attached
To the end of a boat

Drag produced
As wind driven boat

Pulls it along
The roughest water

Will cause
Boat's hyper dynamic

Pointed bow or stern
To face into the wind

The oncoming
Wind–blown water

And the windows of heaven
Were opened

And the rain was upon
The Earth forty days

And forty nights

The windows of heaven
Were opened

When they find out
We are here

For Nuhun Gemisi

Nuhun Gemisi

Without such a device
A wave can hit the boat

Turn it sideways
To the wind and waves

Next wind impacting
The side of the boat

Will have a greater
Likelihood of rolling boat over

Sea anchors
Drogue stones

Prevent this

Mighty anchors of stone
1500 meters above sea level

Mighty anchors of stone

Here we are
In the Valley of the Eight

The Valley of the Eight

Stones
Found on the hillsides

Of these valleys

Southwest of Mt. Ararat

How did they end up here?

So high

Rising into the heavens

Many of the stones
Have crosses on them

8 crosses

Byzantine
Armenian

That curve outwards
At the top

Engraved after stones rediscovered

Probably by crusaders
Armenians

The name of the village
Arzap or Arzep

Possibly comes
From the Turkish

"Arz zapt"

Which means
To capture the Earth

Or possibly further back
From Semite

"In esetz tsap"

Can be translated

To cling to the Earth

Cling to the Earth

They point to
Mt. Ararat

13 miles away

Which rises
Into the mist

Into the mist

Stones in front
Of very old stone house

In a flat open field

Engraved on one of them

A rainbow
Over eight people

A rainbow

Half of them
Have long hair

Half of them
Long beards

6 of them
Are smaller

Then the other two

Noah and Naameh

She is looking down

Eyes closed

Maybe she died first

Both have closed eyes

Bowed heads

Another stone

A boat on top of a wave

Quite a sight

So high up here
In the mountains

No lakes or seas

A boat on top of a wave

Here we are
In the Valley of the Eight

The Valley of the Eight

When on the seventh day
He set forth a dove

And released it

No perch was visible
So it came back to him

He set forth a swallow
And released it

No perch was visible
So it circled back to him

He set forth the raven

And released it

Beat its wings

Flew off

It never came back

It never came back

They point to
Mt. Ararat

Which rises into the mist

★★★

She is awakened
By the familiar pip

Of her cell phone

My daughter Claire
37 years old

Director of Graduate Studies

Biblical archeology

Syro -Palestine archeology

Ancient Israelite

Religious and social history

Greek Bible College

Tall woman
Muscular

Hell of a climber

Been up Mt. Ararat
Many times

The familiar pip
Of her cell phone

For Nuhun Gemisi

2:30 am

Who would be texting her
The middle of the night?

It's from Devrim Akar

In Turkey

Everyone calls him Dev

Forgot 6 hour time difference

Daytime in Turkey

When she reads
The text

Suddenly wide awake

We have found Noah's Ark
I am standing next to it
On Mt. Ararat
What are we to do?

Nuhun Gemisi

Noah's Ark

They point to
Mt. Ararat

13 miles away

Which rises
Into the mist

Rises into the mist

And the Lord was sorry
That He had made humankind
On the Earth

And it grieved Him
To His Heart

So the Lord said

"I will blot out
From the Earth

The human beings
I created

People together
With animals and creeping things

And birds
Of the air

I am so sorry
That I made them"

What are we to do?

My Born Again Christian daughter

Creationist archeologist

God's purpose
Was to make me whole

I pray God may use
My family
For Christ and His Kingdom

What are we to do?

Thinks that the message
Should be taken seriously

It's not April 1ˢᵗ
Or New Year's Eve

Dev would not joke
About this

Not about this

Met him
A few times in Turkey

Knows him quite well

He is their guide there

Also rescues lost climbers
For Turkish government

Reputation for drinking

But he wouldn't lie
About something like this

He wouldn't lie
In the sight

But Noah found favor
In the sight

Of the Lord

These are the descendants
Of Noah

A righteous man

Blameless in his generation

Noah walked with God

Three sons

Shem
Ham
Japheth

Now the Earth
Was corrupt

In God's sight

And the Earth
Was filled with violence

"Now I am going
To destroy them

Along with the Earth

Build yourself an ark
Of cypress wood

What are we to do?
The waters of the Flood
Were upon the Earth

And all the fountains
Of the deep

Were broken up

And the windows of heaven
Were opened

What are we to do?

Take a lot of photos
And stay in touch

And Dev does
But does not send them

Hurried down the mountain
As it is getting dark

Next morning
She calls AIR

Ark Is Real Ministries

In Hong Kong

Her partners
And sponsors

For 6 years

Born Again like Claire

Informed at once
To investigate

The great news

Huang Jin

The director
Of AIR

Does not doubt it either

God is guiding us Claire

I truly believe that

Because of our faith

No kind of human habitation
So high up

On the mountain

God is guiding us Claire

They find the wood

They find the wood

We have to go back to Turkey Claire

To Mt. Ararat

Doomsday Mountain

Find the wood

Claire calls me

Daddy we found the ark!

How do know that Claire?

My faith Daddy

But we're going to
Investigate the find

Have all details confirmed

Before releasing
Big news to the world

Find the wood

A righteous man

Blameless in his generation

A boat on top of a wave

Quite a sight

So high up here
In the mountains

No lakes or seas

A boat on top of a wave

Rises into the mist

I need you to take Jack

I may be gone a few weeks

Is he going to camp?

No, he says he'll keep busy

I wish he'd go to church

His psycho-alcoholic father
Totally confused him

Changed his mind everyday

Undoes everything I try to do with him

All he cares about is his Xbox

Claire's ex a successful contractor

Has 20 year old girlfriend

Jack can stay with me

A challenge
At times

But a good kid
At heart

20 minute car ride away

Now the Earth
Was corrupt

In God's sight

Thank you Daddy

I thank God for you

Everyday

He set forth the raven

And released it

Beat its wings

Flew off

It never came back

It never came back

★★★

Here we are
In the Valley of the Eight

The Valley of the Eight

When they find out
We are here

For Nuhun Gemesi

Nuhun Gemesi

Noah's Ark

They point to
Mt. Ararat

13 miles away

Doomsday Mountain

Which rises
In the mist

Rises into the mist

Doomsday Mountain

The name of the village
Arzap or Arzep

Possibly comes
From the Turkish

"Arz zapt"

Which means
To capture the Earth

Or possibly further back
From Semite

"In esetz tsap"

Can be translated

To cling to the Earth

Cling to the Earth

Estimated flood narratives

From around the world

6000 different accounts

American historian and missionary
Dr. Aaron Smith of Greensborough

Counts 80,000 stories

In 72 languages
About the Flood

70,000 include a boat

In 1951
Spends 12 days

40 companions

To no purpose
Ice cap of Ararat

"Although we found
No trace of Noah's Ark"

Declares later

"My confidence
In the Biblical description

Of the Flood

Is no whit less

We shall go back

We shall go back"

Noah walked with God

Encouraged by Dr. Smith

Young Greenland explorer

Jean de Riquer

Climbs volcanic peak
In 1952

Comes back with nothing

Comes back with nothing

My confidence
In the Biblical description

Of the Flood

Is no whit less

No whit less

80,000 stories

In 72 languages
About the Flood

70,000 include a boat

We shall go back

How did they end up here

So high

Rising into the heavens

Little village
In Turkey

Now called Arzep

Also called

Sagliksuyu

Or Sa Lik Suxu

Acid water in Turkish

Stories of the Flood

Found throughout the world

Old legends
And myths

Most include narrative
Of people being saved

In a boat

Strange if these stories
Come out of pure imagination

Independent of each other

2000 to 3000 years old

Accounts full of
Local differentiation

But the essence
Is the same

The essence
Is the same

All point to idea

There really was at one time
In history of mankind

A great flood

Is no whit less

No whit less

In Sumerian account

Noah is called Ziusudru

Xisuthros in Greek

80,000 stories

In 72 languages

In India
There is a story

In which Noah
Is known as Manu

Ancient Greece
Has a flood story

They conquered Mesopotamia
Around 330 BC

Unclear if they took
Mesopotamian stories

And altered
To fit their own mythology

Or if they had
Own story of the Flood

The Mesopotamian Noah
Is Utnapishtim

Ancient Greek myth
Of Deucalion

Son of Prometheus

Name means
The Extra Wise

King of Phthia in Thessaly

When Zeus
Punishes mankind

By creating a flood

Deucalion
And his wife Pyrrha

Sail in a chest for 9 days

Rivers run in torrents

Seas flood the coastal plan

Engulf foothills with spray

Wash everything clean

Only survivors
After the 9th day

Chest lands
On a mountain Parnassus

The two understand
That "mother" is Gaia

The mother of all living things

And the "bones" to be rocks

They throw the rocks
Behind their shoulders

And the stones form people

The stones form people

Their son Hellen
Becomes father of the Greeks

The Hellenes

Greek-Noah mountain chain

Highest peak 8,061 feet

Considered the home
Of Apollo

And the Muses

Oracular city of Delphi

Is no whit less

No whit less

And at the end of seven days
In the six hundredth year

Of the life of Noah

The waters of the Flood
Were upon the Earth

And all the fountains
Of the deep

Were broken up

And the windows of heaven
Were opened

Here we are
In the Valley of the Eight

Noah and Naameh
His 3 sons
And their wives

The Valley of the Eight

When they find out
We are here

For Nuhun Gemisi

Nuhn Gemisi

The Chinese account
Of the Flood

Legend asserts
The Chinese are descendants

Of Nu-wah

Ancestor of old

Name bares
Striking resemblance to Noah

Striking resemblance

Survives flood

With wife
And 3 sons

Their wives

Exact same way
Noah did

Word for "ship"
In Chinese

Comes from ancient character

Consists of a ship
And a symbol for eight

Other ancient characters

Oracle Bone

The Remnants of the World

 A Boat Stopped on a Mountain

Common to All

Among the Miao people

Ancient stories
Of the Deluge

Includes story of Creation

The Flood with Noah

Tower of Babel

Miao people
Once governed over

Most of inner China

Driven into the mountains
By the Chinese

Missionary Ernest Truax

Spends most of his life
Working for the Lord

Among these people

Up in the mountains

Collects their old accounts

So it poured 40 days
And in torrents

Then 55 days
Of misting and drizzle

The waters surmounted
The mountains and the ranges

The Deluge ascending
Leapt valley and hollow

An Earth with no Earth
Upon which to take refuge

The people were baffled
Impotent and ruined

Despairing
Horror stricken
Diminished and finished

But the Patriarch Nuah
Was righteous

The Matriarch Gaw Bo-lu-en
upright

Built a boat very wide
Made a ship very vast

Entire family
Comes along

Eight of them

Together with male
And female

Of each kind of animal

When the time was fulfilled
God commanded the waters

The day had arrived
The Flood waters receded

Sent a dove to go forth
And bring again tidings

The flood gad gone down
Into lake and to ocean

Land again inhabited

Fattened cattle become
Sacrifice to the Mighty

The Divine One
Gives them his blessing

Their God bestows
His good graces

212 accounts in different cultures

88% about a family
That is saved

70% tell of a boat

66% blame catastrophe
On Mankind's evil

67% include animals
Being saved

73% a worldwide floor

55% survivors rescued from mountain

Even peoples
Completely isolated geographically

From Bible
Middle Eastern world

Indians of South America
Australian Aborigines

Still have their stories
Of the Great Flood

I am standing next to it
On Mt. Ararat
What are we to do?

For Nuhun Gemisi

Nuhun Gemesi

They point to
Mt. Ararat

Doomsday Mountain

13 miles away

Which rises
Into the mist

Rises into the mist

And the Lord was sorry
That He had made humankind
On the Earth

And it grieved Him
To His Heart

So the Lord said

"I will blot out
From the Earth

The human beings
I created

People together
With animals and creeping things

And birds
Of the air

I am so sorry
That I made them"

★★★

We have found Noah's Ark
I am standing in front of it
On Mt. Ararat
What are we to do?

For Nuhun Gemisi

Nuhun Gemisi

Noah's Ark

They point to
Mt. Ararat

13 miles away

Which rises
Into the mist

Rises into the mist

The circumference of the mountain
Is enormous

If one were to walk
Around it

50 miles

Stands alone

So one can see
Its magnificent peak

From far away

Mighty and beautiful

Attracts visitors

Frightens the locals

Know how dangerous
It is

Caught in sudden snowstorm

Fall into a glacier

Walk around it

50 miles

All of the stories

How dangerous

Impossible to climb

The Holy Mountain

Doomsday Mountain

Also called the Maternal Mountain

The Mountain of Pain

What are we to do?

But Noah found favor
In the sight

Of the Lord

These are the descendants
Of Noah

A righteous man

Blameless in his generation

Noah walked with God

Now the Earth
Was corrupt

In God's sight

And the Earth
Was filled with violence

The whole Earth
Flooded for about a year

Even highest mountains
Covered with water

But some mountains
Could have emerged

By continental plates
Gliding over each other

Raising vast lands

Explosions of volcanos

Mountains of lava

Part of Mt. Ararat

Seems to have been formed
Underwater

Pillow lava

The same fossils
Of sea animals and plants

Found on
Other volcanic mountains

In the area

Have not been found here

 Believed by geologists

Upper part of mountain

Wasn't there

Until after Noah's time

Due to volcanic eruptions

This is why
Claire is excited

Dev's find
Of wooden structure

Under ice and lava rocks

At height of almost
14,000 feet

Suggests upper part
Of the volcano

Came into existence

After Noah

But how did he find it?

And did he really find it?

And why now?

Many have claimed
To have found the Ark

I'm interested
Because I'm a semi-retired archeologist

We never really retire

Chairman Emeritus
Cornell Institute of
Archeology and Material Studies

CIAMS

Coordinated archeological activities

At Cornell here in Ithaca, New York

Expeditions to Israel, Syria, Egypt,
Peru, Chile, Greenland, Ireland, Canada

I'm most notorious
For co-discovering

A potential second Viking site
In North America

But how did he find it?

And did he really find it?

And why now?

Many have claimed
To have found the Ark

"My confidence
In the Biblical description

Of the Flood

Is no whit less

We shall go back

We shall go back"

Noah walked with God

Now God loved this man
For his righteousness

Yet he not only
Condemned these other men

For their wickedness

But determined to destroy
The whole race of mankind

And to make another race
That should be pure

From wickedness

An Ark of 4 stories

Three hundred cubic feet

50 cubits broad

And 30 cubits high

Now this Ark
Had firm walls

And a roof

And was braced
With cross beams

So that it could not
In any way be drowned

Or overborne by the violence
Of the water

In the six hundredth year
Of Noah's government

Two thousand six hundred
And fifty six years

From Adam

And to make another race
That should be pure

Stories of the Flood

Found throughout the world

Old legends
And myths

Most include narrative
Of people being saved

In a boat

Strange if these stories
Come out of pure imagination

Independent of each other

2000 to 3000 years old

Accounts full of
Local differentiation

But the essence
Is the same

The essence
Is the same

All point to idea

There really was at one time
In history of mankind

A great flood

Is no whit less

No whit less

Counts 80,000 stories

In 72 languages

About the Flood

70,000 include a boat

Young French Greenland explorer

Jean de Riquer

Climbs volcanic peak
In 1952

Comes back with nothing

Comes back with nothing

How did they end up here

So high

Rising into the heavens

The name of the village
Arzap or Arzep

Possibly comes
From the Turkish

"Arz zapt"

Which means
To capture the Earth

Or possibly further back
From Semite

"In esetz tsap"

Can be translated

To cling to the Earth

Cling to the Earth

And to make another race
That should be pure

From wickedness

For Nuhun Gemesi

Nuhun Gemesi

What are we to do?

Together with Dev
Claire charged with task

Arranging trip
For the Chinese team

To travel to Turkey

They find the wood

A righteous man

Blameless in his generation

A rainbow
Over eight people
A rainbow

Half of them
Have long hair

Half of them
Long beards

6 of them
Are smaller

Then the other two

Noah and Naameh

She is looking down

Eyes closed

A boat on top of a wave

Quite a sight

So high up here
In the mountains

No lakes or seas

A boat on top of a wave

Rises into the mist

Claire swings by

To drop Jack off

Old gray Toyota Camry

Bumper stickers

AS A FORMER FETUS
I OPPOSE ABORTION

JESUS IS MY PASSWORD

Green zephyr V neck tank top
And blue jeans

Has her mother's family's
Big boned genes

Rattles her keys

Jack

Skinny
Blond hair

Metal Head baseball cap
An erring

Holding his X Box
And a duffel bag

Doesn't smile much

Hey Jack
Maybe you can show me some

Of those games

Ok. Sure

What's your favorite?

Favorite what?

Game?

I don't know
A bunch

Maybe we can build some birdhouses

Birdhouses?

Like we used to

That was a long time ago Grandpa

Remember that Osprey box
And we saw them flying above us

Gliding

Sort of

What makes you think
You found the Ark?

You didn't find the Ark Mom
There is no Ark

Maybe you'll come to Turkey
With me one day Jack
It's the Lord's Land

That would be exciting
Not!

What does Huang think?
Does he think it could be it?

The Director of Ark is Real Ministries

AIR

Well we wouldn't be going
If he didn't think this is something

Huang Jin

Decades long obsession
With finding the Ark

Read a news article
In the 1970s

Reporting that
A satellite photo

Taken of Mt. Ararat

Showed a shadow
That could be Noah's Ark

Stories like this
Are frequent

Many have claimed
To have found Noah's Ark

A shadow
That could be Noah's Ark

How did Dev find it?

Where on the mountain is it?

That's a secret
Otherwise there will be nothing left of the site
Looters

A shadow
That can be Noah's Ark

There's something up there

You didn't find the Ark Mom
There is no Ark

I saw the video footage that Dev took
I saw it

Camera enters a hole

About two meters down

A wooden staircase

Old beams of wood
At the top

Wooden nails

Locals say
They were used to tie the animals

And under the ice
There are 2 walls

17 feet high

Wooden beams
At the top

How did Dev find it?
Why now?

We don't know

A shadow
That could be Noah's Ark

Don't let him be on his X Box all the time

Mom! Enough!

Why don't you build some birdhouses with Grandpa?
Jack?

Here we are
In the Valley of the Eight

The Valley of the Eight

When they find out
We are here

For Nuhun Gemisi

Nuhun Gemesi

Noah's Ark

They point to
Mt. Ararat

The Mountain of Pain

★★★

And the water pours down
40 entire days

Until it becomes
15 cubits higher than the Earth

Then the rain ceases
The water begins to abate

After 150 days

70th day
Of the seventh month

Subsides

Arks rests
On a certain mountain

In Armenia

Which when Noah understands
He opens it

Opens it

And seeing
A small piece of land

Some cheerful hopes
Of deliverance

But a few days later
When the waters decrease

To a greater degree

He sends forth

A raven

Sends forth

A raven

As desirous
To learn

Whether any part
Of the Earth

Is left

And whether
He might go out of the Ark

With safety

But the raven

Finding all the land
Still overflows

Returns to Noah again

Returns

★★★

Now God loved this man
For his righteousness

Yet he not only
Condemned these other men

For their wickedness

But determined to destroy
The whole race of mankind

And to make another race
That should be pure

From wickedness

An Ark of 4 stories

Three hundred cubic feet

50 cubits broad

And 30 cubits high

Now this Ark
Had firm walls

And a roof

And was braced
With cross beams

So that it could not
In any way be drowned

Or overborne by the violence
Of the water

In the six hundredth year
Of Noah's government

Two thousand six hundred
And fifty six years

From Adam

And to make another race
That should be pure

Many have claimed
To have found it

A shadow
That could be Noah's Ark

You may want to know about
Bishop Theophilus

Of Antioch
In Northern Syria

180 AD

"And of the Ark
The remains are
To this day

To be seen
In the Arabian Mountains"

The historian
Faustus of Byzantium

A Greek
Wrote about Armenian history

Placed the Ark
In the Gordian Mountains

In the center of Gorduka

St. James
Bishop of Nisibis

Now Nusaybin

Tries in vain
To find the Ark

Legend has it

He was rewarded
A piece of it

By an angel

There have been earthquakes

Volcanic eruptions

One of them

Threw a sixth
Of Mount Ararat

In the air

Leaving a gorge

Ahera Gorge

Northeast side of mountain

A great explosion

Jesus' time

Or before

Might explain

Why no one knows
Where the Ark is

Because it disappeared

Disappeared

You may want to know about

Bishop Ephiphyianus
Of Salamis

4th century

Believed the Ark
Landed in the Gordian mountains

The remains
Can still be found

Can still be found

One can also see
The altar

That Noah built

To thank God
For his salvation

380 AD

Argues truth
Of Christianity

"Do you suppose
We are unable

To prove our point

When even to this day

The remains of Noah's Ark
Are shown

In the country
Of the Kurds"

A great explosion

Might explain

Why no one knows
Where the Ark is

Because it disappeared

Disappeared

William of Rubruck

1255

Franciscan monk

Sent by Louis iX
Of France

To the Mongolian emperor

Writes

"Near this city Naxua

There is a mountain
Of which it is said

Here lies Noah's Ark

The one is larger
Than the other

And the Araxes River

Flows at the foot of them

There is a city
They call Cemanum

When translated
Means "eight"

Named after
The eight people

That came out
Of the Ark

And who built it

Many have tried
To climb the mountain

But have not been able to

An old man
Gave me a good reason

Why not
To try climbing it

The mountain is called
Massis

Mother of the Earth"

Here lies Noah's Ark

Many have claimed
To have found it

A shadow
That could be Noah's Ark

Statements
From many travelers

Over the ages

Quoting people
Who say

"It is up there
On Mount Ararat"

Sometimes

A black spot

On one of the sides
Of the mountain

Is pointed out

Said to be the Ark

Turns out to be
Projection of rocks

Knowledge of the position
Of the Ark

Gradually disappears

Disappears

After volcanic eruption

During time of Jesus

Or centuries after

Blasting one side of the mountain

Devastates whole area

You may want to know about
Sir John Mandeville

1322 to 1356

Travels around the world

Tells that people
Went from Erzerum

To a mountain
Called Sadissocolle

"And there beside
Is another mountain

Called Ararat

The Jews call it
Taneez

Where Noah's ship rested
And still is upon
That mountain

And men may see it afar
In clear weather

Men may see it

That mountain
A full seven miles high

Men say
They have seen

And touched the ship
And put their fingers

In the part
Where Noah said

"Benedicte"

But they say so
Speak without knowledge

For no one
Can go up to the mountain

For the great
Abundance of snow

Which is always
On the mountain

Both summer
And winter

So that no man
Ever went up

Since the time
Of Noah

Except a monk
Who by God's grace

Brought one of
The planks down

Which is yet in the monastery

At the foot of the mountain
And beside the city

Of Dayne
Which was founded

By Noah

Near which
Is the city of Ani

In which were
One thousand churches"

Many claimed
To have found it

A shadow
That could be Noah's Ark

But Noah found favor
In the sight

Of the Lord

These are the descendants
Of Noah

A righteous man

Blameless in his generation

Noah walked with God

Three sons

Shem
Ham
Japheth

Now the Earth
Was corrupt

In God's sight

And the Earth
Was filled with violence

"Now I am going
To destroy them

Along with the Earth

Build yourself an ark
Of cypress wood
The waters of the Flood
Were upon the Earth

And all the fountains
Of the deep

Were broken up

And the windows of heaven
Were opened

Statements
From many travelers

Over the ages

Quoting people
Who say

"It is up there
On Mount Ararat"

Sometimes

A black spot

On one of the sides
Of the mountain

Is pointed out

Said to be the Ark

Knowledge of the position
Of the Ark

Gradually disappears

Disappears

After volcanic eruption

During time of Jesus

Or centuries after

Blasting one side of the mountain

Devastates whole area

And then you might want to know
About the Dutchman

His name is Jan Janszoon Struys

And he has quite a tale

Travels many countries
Europe and Asia

1647–1672

Thought to be a pirate

Has been captured
Sold as a slave

To a Persian master

Memoirs published
1677 in Holland

1681 in France

On the 30th of June 1670
Arrives at Erivan

City at the foot
Of Mt. Ararat

His master
Intends to sell him

But local inhabitants
Express no desire

To buy him

Gives up hope

Two Carmelite monks
Asks if by chance

This fellow Struys
Is a surgeon

If he has any skill
Along that line

Would give him a case
For which he will be well paid

If he succeeds

If he succeeds

"Sorry, I'm not a surgeon"

Never practiced the art

Do not believe him

Perhaps he does not want
To admit it in front of his master

He looks like a surgeon to me

Take master aside

Says one of them

My brother is suffering
From a hernia

And if your slave
Can cure him

We will make you a present
Of 50 crowns

He looks like a surgeon, don't you think?

Let me see to it
He does not like to boast about himself

Takes Struys aside

Jan, are you aware that this gives you a chance
To buy your freedom?

"But Master, I am not a surgeon"

If you are smart
You will take this opportunity my good Doctor Struys

After thinking about it

Resolves to do everything

His master wishes

Has always treated him decently

And he can't sell him

A miracle is promised

There is one caveat

The patient is near the top of that mountain

What?

Lives as a hermit monk
On Mt. Ararat

Hermitage so far
From the foot of the mountain

Takes seven days to scale it

Seven days

A miracle is promised

A miracle is promised

Everyday
They cover 5 miles

Every night
Find a hut

Where they would sleep

Every morning
The hermit who occupies it

Secures a donkey
And a peasant for them

The peasant to guide them

The donkey to carry
Their provisions

And wood for fires

There are no bushes
Or trees

Or even
A thicket of brambles

No top soil

Clouds they pass through
Dark and thick

Almost plunges
Down a ravine

Snow and wind gusts

Freezing cold

"I'm going to perish here"

But the higher they climb

The more temperate
The air

Climb further

Mildness continues

Arrive at Hermitage

Continue to the cell

Of their patient
The 7th of July

Cell large
Well hewn in rock

Che Gentile da parte tua

Italian

How kind of you

Good hermit tells him

During the 25 years
He has lived here

He's never experienced
A gust of wind

Nor drop
Of rainfall

Up on the summit
Of the mountain

Climate even more tranquil

For nothing ever changes here

That is the reason
The very Ark of Noah

Does not deteriorate

Remains for many centuries

Oh yes it is up there

I've been in it

I've touched it
The face of God

Struys tells him to lie down

Takes his pulse

How long have you been a surgeon for?

"Oh, close to my whole life"

Then I am blessed to have you here

You are a true servant of God

Examines area in question

Finds a rupture
Hernia swelling

The size of a hen's egg

"How long have you been
With this condition?"

Only a month

"Then the cure does not come too late
I will bring you the successful remedy"

Touches the rupture spot

Laughs

"In a week or two
You will be as well as I"

What did you do?
I feel better already

The good monk
Overjoyed

Embraces him

I have been blessed by you

You are a true expert
In your profession

I am so privileged

Thank you

Thank you

How did you do that?

"It's my years of apprenticeship"

How can I repay you?

"Just put in a good word for me
With you know who"

His sacred vows prevent him
From giving a rich present

Has nothing more precious
Than a cross

Attached to a silver chain

"Though if you do have 50 crowns"

Removes it
From his neck

Gives it to Struys

"Oh, thank you.Very pretty"

Consists of little fragment of wood
Of reddish brown

And with it a little piece of rock

That is a piece of the very Ark of Noah

And with it a little piece of rock

On which

The Ark came to rest

It is worth a lot

Such a high value
Did he attribute

To these pieces
Of wood and rock

In his judgment

Too rich if Struys
Keeps them

Would he be willing
To take them to St. Peter's Rome

You will be very well paid
I can promise you that

Gives him a letter

His real name is Domingo Alessandro

Son of one the wealthiest families
In Rome

The man cured me
Of a serious hernia

And I am therefore
Greatly in his debt

In return for his benevolence
I have presented to him

A cross
Of a piece of wood

From the Ark of Noah

I myself
Have entered the Ark

And with my own hands
Cut from the wood

Of one of the compartments

And also gave him
A piece of stone

Which I personally chipped
From the rock

On which the Ark rests

I testify to be true
As true as I am

In fact alive here
In my sacred hermitage

2nd of July
1670 Mt. Ararat

Domingo Alessandro of Rome

Carries these holy relics

With donkey
And a guide

Follows same route
As before

Ice laden clouds
Hang over a rough wind

Snow blowing everywhere

Slippery
And steep

Almost plunges

Toward the foot
Of the mountain

Wind and rain
And sleet

Treacherous pathway

Vows
Never to return

Never to return

Neither the Ark
Nor the rock that cradles it
As my hermit's testimony asserts
Would have an attraction
Sufficient enough
To draw me there again

Many claimed
To have found it

A shadow
That could be Noah's Ark

★★★

Can you keep a secret?

The Kurdish old man

Asks the boy

A 300 year old secret

Ali Kaderi Sunay

Uncle of the boy's mother

Can you keep a secret?

A 300 year old secret

About a cave

In the Valley of the Spirits

A cave

High up on the Mountain

God's Mountain

Can you keep a secret?

Promise me

No one from the outside

May know

What I am about to tell you

No one may know

It is only for us

300 years ago

There was a shepherd
Named Abbas

Tending his sheep

As usual

On the mountain
Ararat

Only for us

Because the soil is barren

Leads his flock

Higher and higher

Up the mountain

Until he discovers

A new place

Strange, mysterious

A cave in the Valley of the Spirit

High up

On the mountain

Strange and mysterious

Looks like
A huge wooden building

With partitions

And clay pots

What is this doing

All the way up here?

No one
Can live up here

Old beams of wood
At the top

Wooden nails

And under the ice
There are 2 walls

17 feet high

Wooden beams
At the top

Even finds some wheat

Take some of it

And a piece of the wood

Back to his place

Tells no one

No one

Protects the location

Hides the entrance

He thinks he will return

But he never does

Never does

The wheat he brings down

Brought to Iran

Other side of border

Tries to sow it

Grow it

But too dry

After all of these
Thousands of years

Thousands of years

He thinks he knows
What he saw

But that can't be true

 Can it?

Tries to go back again

But dies
Before he can

Fulfill his dream

But the story
Handed down

To his great, great, great, grandson

Me

Kader

Kept secret
For 70 years

And now is telling
The boy

You have a glow
About you

Can you keep a secret?

There was an earthquake

And volcanic eruptions

1840

And the structure
Was moved

No one
Has found it since

No one has found it

But maybe one day

You will

Promise me

No one from the outside
May know

No one may know

Shhhh

★★★

And the Lord hearkened
To the voice of Noah

And the Lord
Remembered him

And a wind
Passed over the Earth

And the waters
Were still

And the Ark rested

And the fountains of the deep
And the windows of heaven

Were stopped

And the waters decreased
In those days

And the Ark rested
Upon the mountain
Of Ararat

Rested upon the mountain
Of Ararat

And the Lord hearkened
To the voice of Noah

And said to him

"When thou shall have completed
A full year
Thou shall go forth"

And at the revolution
Of the year

When a full year
Was completed

Of Noah's dwelling
In the Ark

The waters were dried
Off the earth

And Noah put off
The covering of the Ark

And the day came
That the Lord told them

To go out
And they all went from the Ark

The sons of Japeth
Spread towards the west
And got Europe

Shem's descendants
Got what later became
The Arabic lands

And Ham's descendants
Got Egypt and Africa

Here we are
In the Valley of the Eight

The Valley of the Eight

When they find out
We are here

For Nuhun Gemesi

Nuhun Gemesi

They point to
Mt. Ararat

13 miles away

Which rises
Into the mist

Rises into the mist

He calls it
A secret source

News from other people

But he won't tell them

Dev won't tell them

A secret source

Of a secret location

He got the secret news
And then he went there

And then he went there

They think
To verify

So he went there first

After he went there
He texted Claire

Very excited

On the mountain
For many years

And he hadn't seen
Such a structure before

A rainbow
Over eight people

A rainbow

Half of them
Have long hair

Half of them
Long beards

6 of them
Are smaller

Then the other two

Noah and Naameh

She is looking down

Eyes closed

The name of the village
Arzap or Arzep

Possibly comes
From the Turkish

"Arz zapt"

Which means
To capture the Earth

Or possibly further back
From Semite

"In esetz tsap"

Can be translated

To cling to the Earth

Cling to the Earth

2:30 am

Who would be texting her
The middle of the night?

It's from Devrim Akar

In Turkey

Everyone calls him Dev

Forgot 6 hour time difference

Daytime in Turkey

When she reads
The text

Suddenly wide awake

We have found Noah's Ark
I am standing next to it
On Mt. Ararat
What are we to do?

Nuhun Gemisi

Noah's Ark

But this secret source

Who told him
That he might find it

Why didn't he
Come forward before?

In the past
Many mountain people

Went to the top

And some of the seekers
Went inside

And told the news
To their families

The secret

To their sons
Grandchildren

Some families
Might have the secret

But the grandson
Hadn't gone there yet

A cave

High up on the Mountain

God's Mountain

Can you keep a secret?

Promise me

No one from the outside

May know

What I am about to tell you

No one may know

It is only for us

Claire sends me
A snippet of video

From Turkey

Inside a cave

Secret location

We can't tell anyone
Where it is

We can't tell anyone

It's a secret

A secret

Under the ice
Is wood

With a beam
Protruding out

There is also
Tenon construction

Of the wall

Artificial

Or man-made

Another space
Is L-shaped

First space discovered

Matches well
With other spaces discovered

Huang Jin

The director
Of AIR

Does not doubt it either

God is guiding us Claire

I truly believe that

Because of our faith

No kind of human habitation
So high up

On the mountain

God is guiding us Claire

They find the wood

They find the wood

We have to go back to Turkey Claire

To Mt. Ararat

Doomsday Mountain

Find the wood

Claire calls me

Daddy we found the ark!

How do know that Claire?

My faith Daddy

But we're going to
Investigate the find

Have all details confirmed

Similar tenon construction

Might have been
Originally box shaped room

But now heavily
Decomposed

Room number 3
Buried under

Ice and volcanic surroundings

Decomposed by surroundings

I can clearly see wood

Room 5
16 feet high

Team had to be
Lowered down

Through a broken opening
To get inside

All walls
Made of wood

Space not box shaped

Walls not vertical

But curved
And inclined

With dimensions
Of 3 feet high

18 inches wide

Presumably leads
To other spaces

But the team
Didn't go any further

Lack of oxygen

Claire texts me

Dev says he saw it
In a dream

A revelation

A vision

But we have all

Been praying too

For the Lord's guidance

A tradition
In Kurdish community

Written message
Found in a jar

Estate of somebody

Last words
Of a dying person

Leads his flock

Higher and higher

Up the mountain

Until he discovers

A new place

Strange, mysterious

A cave in the Valley of the Spirit

High up

On the mountain

Strange and mysterious

Looks like
A huge wooden building

With partitions

And clay pots

What is this doing

All the way up here?

No one
Can live up here

Old beams of wood
At the top

Wooden nails

And under the ice
There are 2 walls

17 feet high

Wooden beams
At the top

Even finds some wheat

A cave

High up on the Mountain

God's Mountain

Can you keep a secret?

Promise me

No one from the outside

May know

What I am about to tell you

No one may know

It is only for us

Last words
Of a dying person

Last words

Many people
Of the mountain

Maybe some
Entered the cave

Told the secret
To their son

Their grandchildren

And they handed it down

Handed it down

He calls it
A secret source

News from other people

But he won't tell them

Dev won't tell them

A secret source

Of a secret location

He got the secret news
And then he went there

And then he went there

AIR invites
Turkish representatives

To inspect the find

Once they verify it themselves

Not the first time
People have claimed

To have found the Ark

But how did he find it?

And did he really find it?

And why now?

Many have claimed
To have found the Ark

"My confidence
In the Biblical description

Of the Flood

Is no whit less

We shall go back

We shall go back"

Noah walked with God

Press release from Turkey

GREAT NEW FIND

Team finally succeeded
In uncovering

A large petrified
Wooden structure

Carried a few samples

Down from the mountain

For analysis

On the occasion

They measure
The wooden structure

The part they uncovered

38 feet long
8.5 feet wide

Now their research
Has begun to pay off

Such a big wooden structure
Has never before

Been discovered
On the mountain

Never before

Has there been proof
So far

That it exists

That it exists

Even though eye witnesses

Over the years

Told about similar discoveries

But now the team
Could video the location

The secret location

Document their find

But first they
Had to remove

All volcanic ash
Covering the place

And the Lord was sorry
That He had made humankind
On the Earth

And it grieved Him
To His Heart

So the Lord said

"I will blot out
From the Earth

The human beings
I created

People together
With animals and creeping things

And birds
Of the air

I am so sorry
That I made them"

What are we to do?

Once ashes removed
Wood surface structure appear

Assisting the team

Mountain climber
And guide Devrim Akar

Dr. Almet Ozbok
Geologist
Kahramanmaras Sutcu Iman University

Dr. Ozlem Cevik
Archeologist
Trakya University

Professor Orkay Bell
Director of Eurasian Archeology
University of Istanbul

Interest of the press
And others

Considerable
In Turkey, Hong Kong

Other parts of Asisa

But the news
Doesn't register

In the west

Doesn't register

Nobody seems
To realize

The polite Chinese
And Turkish friends

Made such a
Monumental discovery

A wooden object
So high upon Mt. Ararat

They're not westerners

They're creationists

Fanatics

Need prominent archeologist
From the west

With objectivity

No religious agenda

Objectivity

Now God loved this man
For his righteousness

Yet he not only
Condemned these other men

For their wickedness

But determined to destroy
The whole race of mankind

And to make another race
That should be pure

From wickedness

An Ark of 4 stories

Three hundred cubic feet

50 cubits broad

And 30 cubits high

Now this Ark
Had firm walls

And a roof

And was braced
With cross beams

So that it could not
In any way be drowned

Or overborne by the violence
Of the water

In the six hundredth year
Of Noah's government

Two thousand six hundred
And fifty six years

From Adam

And to make another race
That should be pure

Stories of the Flood

Found throughout the world

Old legends
And myths

Most include narrative
Of people being saved

In a boat

Claire texts me again

God unpacked all my baggage
And clarified my doubts

God instilled within me
A new passion

And joy that
I always wanted

I realize that the purpose
Of my study is not knowledge

Or skills

But God's purpose
Was to make me whole

I'm at the house
With Jack

I watch him
Play on his Xbox One

He's trying to show me
The hang of it

While he plays
Some of the metal music he likes

Hatebreed
Faith No More

The game is

CALL OF DUTY
BLACK OPS III

A dark future

Where a new breed

Of black ops soldier emerges

The lines blurred

Between humanity

And the cutting edge technology

Of robotics

The future combat technology

A world facing upheaval
From climate change

And new technologies

Infiltrate base in
Ethiopia

To rescue hostage

From the tyrannical
NRE

Assisted by
Commander John Taylor

And his team
Of cybernatically enhanced soldiers

How do you like it Grandpa?

I think that board games
Are more for me

Or helping you
With your coin collection

Do you still collect?

No

Do you still play basketball?

No, not really

Hey do you want to see
That Osprey nesting box we made

4 years ago?

Not really

We can drive over

A wooden platform
On a pole that we put up

By a pond

Hunt by diving
To water surface

30 to 100 feet

Gripping pads
On their feet

To help them
Pluck fish

From the water

Curved claw

Carry them a great distance

A great distance

Orient the fish head first
To east wind resistance

We made it together

Don't you want to see it?

Not now
Maybe when I'm back from camping

Camping?

Yeah in a few days

With a bunch of friends

Who are the friends?

You wouldn't know them
They're pretty new

Where are you camping?

Taughamock

Another text from Claire
In Turkey

We want Ernie
To join the team

I can't ask you
Because you are my father

And I need someone for Jack

Ernest Beard
Classmate of mine from Columbia

Together we discovered
The second Viking find in North America

Nickname that stuck:
The Space Archeologist

He pioneered satellites
To find sites

Made all of these discoveries
In Egypt

And then the Viking thing

You sure you want to ask Ernie?

Why wouldn't I?
He's good

I don't know
He can be difficult

We need his credibility
And reputation

I am not sure
It is a good idea

How's Jack?

He's fine

He wants to go camping

Not in the park
With the gorges

They dive
Off of them

I think so

I don't like these new friends

They're trouble

Bad parents

No church

All that death metal

His brain dead father
Ignores this problem

One of them lit trash cans
In a park on fire

They have no guidance
From their parents

No church

Jack parties with them

I don't like them

I tell Jack
What she said

Says the crazy woman
Who climbs mountains in Turkey

Looking for a fucking ark?

Mom's losing it
You know that

She thinks dinosaurs
Co-existed with people

That dinosaur researchers
Are liars

That there was a race of Giants
And the Smithsonian covers it up

All that God stuff
Drives me nuts

Well I'm going camping

Fuck her

Grand Canyon

Claire points to it

That was created
By the Biblical Flood

The Deluge

Noah's flood

The dinosaur bones
Are at the bottom

Because they were heavier
And sunk

Heavier and sunk

So high up here
In the mountains

No lakes or seas

A boat on top of a wave

Here we are
In the Valley of the Eight

The Valley of the Eight

When on the seventh day
He set forth a dove

And released it

No perch was visible
So it came back to him

He set forth a swallow
And released it

No perch was visible
So it circled back to him

He set forth the raven

And released it

Beat its wings

Flew off

It never came back

It never came back

★★★

We read the Nordic Sagas
For possible clues

Possible clues

The Sagas believed
To be real history

Not fiction

According to
Icelandic Sagas

Erik the Red's Saga

Saga of the Greenlands

Plus chapters
Of the Houksbok

And the Flatey Book

The Norse started
To explore lands

West of Greenland

Vikings

Only a few years
After the Greenland settlement

985 AD

While sailing from
Iceland to Greenland

Migration fleet
Of 400–700 settlers

25 ships

A merchant named
Bjarni Herjolfsson

And his crew

Blown off course

Wind and fog

3 days of being lost

Sees land
West of the fleet

West of the fleet

Only interested
In finding his father's farm

This does not
Fit the description

Of Greenland

Describes his discovery
To Leif Erikson

Who explores
In more detail

Plants small settlement
15 years later

Sagas describe
3 separate areas discovered

During the exploration

Helluland

Which means

"Land of the Flat Stones"

Markland

"The Land of the Forests"

Definitely of interest

To settlers
Of Greenland

Where there are
Few trees

And Vinland

"The Land of the Wine"

Found somewhere
South of Markland

Old Norse word Saga
Is cognate to English ""say"

Meaning in Old Norse

"What is Said"

Tale

Story

Narrative

Originally transmitted
Orally

Very words
And deeds of the ancestors

9th to 11th centuries

2 centuries
Before being written down

They went on board
And sailed out to sea

Once more

Once more

They found
A second country

And again
Dropped anchor

Put out a boat

Went ashore

Level and wooded

With broad white beaches

Wherever they went

And a gently sloping
Shoreline

Leif said:

"I shall give this
Country a name

That fits with its
Natural character

And call it Markland"

The Land of the Forests

Ernie uses
WorldView 3 satellite sensor

Eyes in the Sky

We're going to find us
Some Vikings Sam!

They can't hide from us

Or I'm not
The Space Archeologist!

Multi-payload
Super spectral
High resolution

Commercial satellite sensor

Operating at altitude
Of 400 miles

WorldView 3

Eyes in the Sky

Provides 31cm panchromatic resolution

1.24 m multispectral resolution

3.7 m short wave infrared resolution

Ernie's used it

To locate lost Egyptian cities

Temples and tombs

Eyes in the Sky

On Canada now

Newfoundland

Space based surveillance

In barren desert landscapes

And regions overrun
By tall grasses

Trees

Eyes in the Sky

Searching for Viking settlements

Location Location Location Sam!

Thousands of miles

Infrared images

Canadian Arctic
To New England

From 400 miles in space

Show possible
Manmade shapes

Under discolored vegetation

Remnants of structure

Alter surrounding soil

Change the amount

Of moisture it retains

Affect the vegetation

Growing directly over it

Using remote sensing

Variations in plant growth

Form a spectral outline

Of what was there

What was there

Centuries earlier

Remnants of structure

Bingo Sam!

Bingo!

There was no land
In sight

The tail wind
Died down

And they were beset
By fogs and north winds

Until they lost
All track of their course

Lost all track of their course

★★★

And they said to Noah

"We are ready to return
To the Lord

Only open for us
So that we may live

And not die"

And Noah answered them

"Behold now
That you see the trouble
Of your souls,

Now also the Lord
Will not listen to you
Neither will He give ear
To you on this day

So that you will not succeed
In your wishes"

And the sons of men approached
In order to break into the Ark

To come in
On account of the rain

For they could not bear
The rain upon them

The rain upon them

And the Lord sent
All of the beasts
And animals that stood
Round the Ark

And the beasts
Overpowered them

And drove them
From that place

And every man went his way

And they again scattered themselves

Upon the face
Of the Earth

The face of the Earth

When they find out
We are here

For Nuhun Gemesi

Nuhun Gemesi

Noah's Ark

They point to
Mt. Ararat

13 miles away

Which rises
Into the mist

Rises into the mist

Frenchman Fernard Navarra

Catalyst for Ark Fever

Latter half

Of 20th century

Writes a book

I FOUND NOAH'S ARK

Creates world- wide sensation

Leads many to believe

He has found the Ark

Even if it is
A shadow under the ice

A shadow under the ice

1939

Serves in the French Army

In the Middle East

In spare time

Climbs mountains

With Armenian refugee
Alim

Once when
On the mountain of Hermon

Alim tells him
Of the holy mountain

Of his native country

Doomsday Mountain

Another man tells Alim

That the Ark
Is up there

The Ark is up there

Next 15 years

Navarra collects
All information

On the Ark
The Deluge

The countries
Neighboring Ararat

1952

Travels to Turkey

Onward to Iran border
620 miles away

Reaches eastern most
Part of Turkey

Accompanied by locals

Turkish soldiers

Climbs to the top
Of the mountain

Top of the mountain

16,853 feet

Attempts to reach the place
On western side

That local monks
Always point to

From the ground

Little black shadow

Where the Ark
Supposedly projects

From the ice

Little black shadow

Arrives fairly close

The "Half Ark"
Sticking out is just rocks

No Ark

Disappointed

But there is another rumor

Diverse accounts

Of the Ark
Lying in a lake

Kep Lake

13,123 feet high

Others from expedition
Desert him

Freezing from the cold

Continues by himself

Perilous

Wind

Fog

Up to Parrot Glacier

2 pm

August 17, 1952

Makes incredible discovery

Incredible discovery

He is alone

On the glacier

That is lying

Shiningly clear
And naked

In the sky
An eagle hovers

Carried by wind

An eagle hovers

Passes a glacier arm

At one side

Can see mass of ice

Streaked with crevasses

At other side

Steep rock wall

And at the bottom
A dark mass

A dark mass

Curves
And straight lines

Encountering
Each other

Object is
Almost 400 feet

Shaped
Like the rail

Of a ship

A ship

What is it?

What can it be?

At this height

Middle of a glacier

And the great waste

Ruins of a ship?

A refuge?

A house?

The wreck
Of an old airplane?

We have to face
What it truly is

The remains of Noah's Ark

Noah's Ark

How did they end up here?

So high

Rising into the heavens

The name of the village
Arzap or Arzep

Possibly comes
From the Turkish

"Arz zapt"

Which means
To capture the Earth

Or possibly further back
From Semite

"In esetz tsap"

Can be translated

To cling to the Earth

Cling to the Earth

And to make another race
That should be pure

From wickedness

For Nuhun Gemesi

Nuhun Gemesi

And the rain
Was still descending

40 days
And 40 nights

And the waters
Prevailed

Upon the Earth

And all flesh
That was upon the Earth

Or in the waters died

Whether man, animals
Beast, creeping things

Birds of the air

And these only remain

Noah and those
That were with him
In the Ark

And these only remain

In the sky
An eagle hovers

Carried by wind

An eagle hovers

We have to face
What it truly is

The remains of Noah's Ark

Noah's Ark

Cannot be anything else

Probably
What is left

Of the flat bottom
Of biblical ship

Probably
What is left

Berosus tells us

People of the Ararat region

In his day

Would break pieces
Of the Ark

To scrape off
The patch covering

The balks they left alone

Remain untouched

Through the ages

Protected by Nature

Opposite steep rock wall

Are enormous blocks

Worked loose

Covering the dark contours

A shadow under the ice

Cannot get down there

Block would crush him

Fixes the place
In this head

Solemnly declares
That he will return

Returns the next year

But feels too ill
And anxious

Maybe due to the height

The year after
American John Libby

Declares he saw
Boat shaped object

In that spot

That spot

Shadow under the ice

Navarra decides
To try again

1955

For the 3rd time

Brings his wife
And 3 sons

So they look like tourists

Not attract
Too much attention

Together with eldest son
11 years old

Climb Ararat
From the west side

Second day

7 am

Reach Kep Lake

Where Navarra
Thought he saw

The Shadow of the Ark
Under the ice

Exhausted

The put up a tent

Now God loved this man
For his righteousness

Yet he not only
Condemned these other men

For their wickedness

But determined to destroy
The whole race of mankind

And to make another race
That should be pure

From wickedness

An Ark of 4 stories

Three hundred cubic feet

50 cubits broad

And 30 cubits high

Now this Ark
Had firm walls

And a roof

And was braced
With cross beams

So that it could not
In any way be drowned

Or overborne by the violence
Of the water

In the six hundredth year
Of Noah's government

Two thousand six hundred
And fifty six years

From Adam

And to make another race
That should be pure

Many have claimed
To have found it

A shadow
That could be Noah's Ark

Navarra feels ill again

Anxiety

Drinks some cognac

During the night

A storm comes on

Wind

Rain

Hail

Blocks of lava
Tumble around them

They're terrified

The next day

He and son Raphael

Reach deep crevice

A shadow
That could be Noah's Ark

Rediscovers
One of the wooden balks

He saw

It has to be the Ark

It has to be

Snowstorm

Almost freeze to death

13 hours

Excavate a real balk
From the ice

A real balk

Get safely down

Visits experts
In Bordeaux

Cairo

Madrid

Study cellular changes

Formation of lignite

Quantity of fossilization

Cambia

Publishes a book

But results
Inconclusive

Doubts of credibility

Both the wood

And the man

Attacks

It's a hoax

He's a liar

Con artist

One of his companions

Alain Seeker

Denies he was on expedition

His son Raphael

Later refuses
To speak about it

Refuses

J. A. de Riquier
From first expedition

Makes serious accusations

Tried to obtain
A piece of wood

From ancient construction

Village below mountain

With intention

To discover it
On the mountain

Turkish lieutenant
Sahup Alaley

Claims to have climbed
Mountain with Navarra

1952

He brought up
Wood with him

So he could make money
On books and photos

Later Carbon 14 tests
Of the wood

Shows it is only
Between 130–1900 years old

Much too young
To be from Noah's Ark

Much too young

The circumference of the mountain
Is enormous

If one were to walk
Around it

50 miles

Stands alone

So one can see
Its magnificent peak

From far away

Mighty and beautiful

Attracts visitors

Frightens the locals

Know how dangerous
It is

Caught in sudden snowstorm

Fall into a glacier

Walk around it

50 miles

All of the stories

How dangerous

Impossible to climb

The Holy Mountain

Doomsday Mountain

Also called the Maternal Mountain

The Mountain of Pain

But Noah found favor
In the sight

Of the Lord

These are the descendants
Of Noah

A righteous man

Blameless in his generation

Noah walked with God

Now the Earth
Was corrupt

In God's sight

And the Earth
Was filled with violence

The whole Earth
Flooded for about a year

Even highest mountains
Covered with water

But some mountains
Could have emerged

By continental plates
Gliding over each other

Raising vast lands

Explosions of volcanos

Mountains of lava

Part of Mt. Ararat

The Mountain of Pain

★★★

Counts 80,000 stories

In 72 languages

About the Flood

70,000 include a boat

The Chinese account
Of the Flood

Legend asserts
The Chinese are descendants

Of Nu-wah

Ancestor of old

Name bares
Striking resemblance to Noah

Striking resemblance

Survives flood

With wife
And 3 sons

Their wives

Exact same way
Noah did

Word for "ship"
In Chinese

Comes from ancient character

Consists of a ship
And a symbol for eight

Other ancient characters

Oracle Bone

The Remnants of the World

A Boat Stopped on a Mountain

A Boat Stopped on a Mountain

"There's something up there"

Something happens to me

1943

Haunts me my whole life

I'm Ed Davis

363rd Army Corps of Engineers

Working out of a base
In Hamadan, Iran

Something happens to me

Building a way station

Into Russia
From Turkey

A supply route

We can see it
Clearly on the horizon

We can see it

"That's where the
Ark landed?"

Badi nods

"My grandfather
Knows where it is

And has gone up there"

In July
His grandfather Abas-Abas

Visits our base

Tells Badi

The ice on Ararat

Is melting

You can see
Part of the Ark

Badi tells me
If I want to see it

They will
Take me there

Take me there

I had done
A favor for their village

Put me in good
With Abas family

Now they have water

Had walk
Two miles to get it

Now they have water

Go to my commanding office

Ask for leave

"It's dangerous up there
You'll get killed"

Gives me R and R
In Tehran

Take the long way

A few days later
We get up early

Drive down along border
As far as Casbeen

Dawn
The next day

We reach foothills
Of Ararat

Village of
Cermanz 'zmz

Means
"Where Noah Planted the Vine"

Grape vines
So thick

At the trunk

Can't reach around them

Very old

And at the end of seven days
In the six hundredth year

Of the life of Noah

The waters of the Flood
Were upon the Earth

And all the fountains
Of the deep

Were broken up

And the windows of heaven
Were opened

And the rain was upon
The Earth forty days

And forty nights

The windows of heaven
Were opened

Badi says
They have a cave

Filled with artifacts

That came from the Ark

Find them

Strewn about a canyon

Below the Ark

Collect them

Keep them from outsiders

Looters

All sacred to them

They show me

Oil lamps

Old style tools

A cage like door

30 to 40 inches

Made of wooden branches

Hard as stone

Hand carved latch on it

Can see wood grain

We sleep

At first light

Put on mountain clothes

Bring up the horses

Leave with seven male members
Abas family

Ride a long time

Tell me
We're going through

A back door

A back door

Secret trail
Used by smugglers

And bandits

Ride along
High cliff

Hard to see

Rain

Fog

Freezing wind

Badi tells me
To be quiet

Russian sentries
Stationed below

Might hear us

Ride in silence

Rest of day

Short whistles
To communicate

With each other

Ride in silence

Until out of trail

Someone from the family

Waiting for us

Takes our horses

We are roped together

Climb on foot

Much higher

Another cave

Next morning
We get up

And wait

Rain lets up

Walk along
A narrow trail

Behind a
Dangerous outcropping

Doomsday Rock

Double back
Around imposing rock formation

Come to a ledge

Enveloped by fog

But suddenly it lifts

Lifts

Sun breaks
Through the clouds

Light shimmers
On the west canyon

My friends
Pray to Allah

They finish

Badi points down

A kind of horseshoe crevasse

"That's Noah's Ark"

But I can't see anything

Can't see

Everything same color
And texture

Then I see it

Rectangular
Manmade structure

Partly covered
By ice and lava rock

Lying on its side

At least 100 feet

Clearly visible

Ice inside it

Looks like it's been

Broken off

Timbers sticking out

Twisted

Clearly visible

Abas points down
The canyon

Another portion of it

Tell me
The Ark broken

Into 3 or 4 pieces

Inside biggest piece

Can see 3 floors

Abas says
There 48 rooms

Cages inside
As small as my hand

We can do down
On ropes in the morning

"And you can touch it"

Next morning

Snowing

Fell all night

Up to our waists

Can't see anything
Down the canyon

The Ark
No longer visible

No longer visible

"We have to leave
It's too dangerous"

After 150 days

70th day
Of the seventh month

Subsides

In Armenia

Which when Noah understands
He opens it

And seeing
A small piece of land

Some cheerful hopes
Of deliverance

But a few days later
When the waters decrease

To a greater degree

He sends forth

A raven

Sends forth

A raven

As desirous
To learn

Whether any part
Of the Earth

Is left

And whether
He might go out of the Ark

With safety

But the raven

Finding all of the land
Still overflows

Returns to Noah again

Returns

★★★

Here we are
In the Valley of the Eight

The Valley of the Eight

When they find out
We are here

For Nuhun Gemisi

Nuhun Gemesi

Noah's Ark

They point to
Mt. Ararat

13 miles away

Which rises
Into the mist

Rises into the mist

Text from Ernie
Istanbul

I don't know why
They need me

Because you're
A mainstream archeologist

Who they feel
Lends this discovery credibility

Yeah yeah
The Space Archeologist

Been starting to search for it too
The Ark

Eyes in the Sky

Eyes in the Sky

You think
They really found it?

I don't know
I've only seen video

They're getting
Carbon 14 dating

I'm skeptical Sam
Very skeptical

They won't
Tell me the location

But I think I know
I know

I'm only doing this for you

Because of Claire

I appreciate that Ernie

You're like family

We've been through the wars Sam

We're survivors

But Noah found favor
In the sight

Of the Lord

These are the descendants
Of Noah

A righteous man

Blameless in his generation

Noah walked with God

Three sons

Shem
Ham
Japeth

Now the Earth
Was corrupt

In God's sight

And the Earth
Was filled with violence

"Now I am going
To destroy them

Along with the Earth

Build yourself an ark
Of cypress wood"

More video from Claire

I can see her, Dev
Huang Jin

And others from AIR

Ark is Real Ministries

God is guiding us Claire

We are being rewarded
For our faith

And perseverance

7 feet down
A wooden staircase

A wooden staircase

Yes

An old staircase
Of wood

Inside space
Old beams of wood

At the top
Wooden nails

Locals say

Used to tie up animals

Under the ice

2 walls

16 feet high

Wooden beams
At the top

Huge structure
But not very wide

Continue to another room

Tilted

Dev doesn't let them
Go in

Very dangerous

Some rocks
Fell down

At the end
A wooden room

Can't get in

But one of them
Fan Li

Crawls through a hole

But can't get out

Dev
Small man

Thick mustache
Late 50s

Helps Fan Li

Says he had chance

To see another huge structure

A space

Huge wooden wall

Very narrow

Can't see the top

Wooden walls
And a ceiling

Could it just be
An old house

Built up
On the mountain

No we call it a vessel

A vessel

Level

Not exactly a room
People can live in

More suited
For animals

Many animals

Of all kinds

As they go deeper

Some of the spaces
Triangular

Room to live in
Wouldn't be triangular

Length of
Longest piece of wood

Over 35 feet

Looks very old

All of it

Because of the tenons

A lot under ice

We've sent a piece of wood
For dating

What is the significance

Of this find?

What will it mean

To the world?

So the Lord said

"I will blot out
From the Earth

The human beings
I created

People together
With animals and creeping things

And birds
Of the air

I am sorry
That I made them"

And to make another race
That should be pure

Stories of the Flood

Found throughout the world

Old legends
And myths

Most include narrative
Of people being saved

In a boat

Strange if these stories
Come out of pure imagination

Independent of each other

2000 to 3000 years old

Accounts full of
Local differentiation

But the essence
Is the same

The essence
Is the same

All point to idea

There really was at one time
In history of mankind

A great flood

Is no whit less

No whit less

Counts 80,000 stories

In 72 languages

About the Flood

70,000 include a boat

And to make another race
That should be pure

From wickedness

An Ark of 4 stories

Three hundred cubic feet

50 cubits broad

And 30 cubits high

Now this Ark
Had firm walls

And a roof

And was braced
With cross beams

So that it could not
In any way be drowned

Or overborne by the violence
Of the water

In the six hundredth year
Of Noah's government

Two thousand six hundred
And fifty six years

From Adam

And to make another race
That should be pure

Call from Claire
In Turkey

Dad the carbon 14 dating
Is 4 to 5 thousand years

That's just right

That's fantastic Claire
Maybe you really found it

I hear Ernie
Is on his way now

He actually arrived
A few hours ago

He wanted to go
To the site this afternoon

Eager to get to work

But they told him
Tomorrow

The weather should be good

Seemed a little peeved

Well you know Ernie
He can be cantankerous

Don't say
I didn't warn you

But he's such
A great archeologist

If we get
His seal of approval

We're in business

This carbon dating
Is already huge

How is Jack?

Plays his games

His music

Goes out with his friends

The band rehearsed
In the garage last night

I had to wear ear plugs

And I have bad hearing

See I don't like
Those friends of his

They're new

I liked his old friends

But Jack says they're boring
And too geeky

The more I say something
The more he sees them

Take Tucker

Which one is he?

Tall, skinny
Red head

Acne

He's older

Cuts school
All the time

Drinks
Probably does drugs

I tell Jack
Not to get in the car with him

If he's drinking
And driving

I want to help Tucker
Because his parents don't

And therefore there must
Be good in his heart

Like Jack

I want to help him

I want to help him

Because Jack likes him

I told him
He could go camping

But no gorge diving

No drinking

Absolutely no drugs

And Tucker is allowed
In our house

If he follows the rules

Proverb 31

God's word says
That he opens her hand
To the poor

And reach out her
Hands to the needy

The Deluge

Noah's flood

The dinosaur bones
Are at the bottom

Because they were heavier
And sunk

Heavier and sunk

Late afternoon
Jack gather his gear

For camping

Tent
Sleeping bag

Water bottle
Food

Hot dogs
Marshmallows

That's a lot of hot dogs

How many of you are going Jack?

9 of us, I think

No gorge diving
Remember

Yeah, right

I will be careful Grandpa
That I promise

When you're back
Maybe we can look at the ospreys

Or build some
Bird boxes

Yeah
Maybe Grandpa

Doorbell rings

Tucker

Tall, stringy red hair
Pimples

Red blood
Pentagram tee shirt

Torn jeans

Grunts something
At me

I think it was hello

Looks in my fridge
Without asking

See you in a few days
Grandpa

Be careful

We will Grandpa

We will

Don't sound like Mom

In the night

A text from Claire

Ernie was missing
In the morning

Missing from camp

I remember
Jack and I

Watching
The mother osprey

Flying around

Hovering

2 feet in length

6 foot wingspan

Soar high
Above their prey

Then dive feet first
Full force

Dive

Into the water

Fully submerged

Brings up its catch

Brings up its catch

Feet have barbed pads

Evolved to help them

Hold slippery fish

Carry the fish head first

For aerodynamic flight

Thunders off

Thunders

★★★

And the rain
Was still descending

Upon the Earth

And it descended
Forty days
And forty nights

And the waters
Prevailed greatly

Upon the Earth

And all flesh
That was upon the Earth died

Whether men, animals
Beast, creeping things
Or birds of the air

And there
Only remained
Noah and those

That were with him
In the Ark

And the waters prevailed
And they greatly increased

And they lifted the Ark
And it was raised from the Earth

And the Ark
Floated upon
The face of the waters

The face of the waters

So that all
Of the living creatures within

Were turned like pottage
In a cauldron

And great anxiety
Seized all the living creatures
That were in the Ark

And the Ark
Was like to be broken

And all the living creatures
That were in the Ark
Were terrified

And the lions roared
And the oxen lowed
And the wolves howled

And every living creature
In the Ark
Spoke and lamented

In its own language
So that their voices
Reached a great distance

A great distance

And Noah and his sons cried
And wept in their troubles
They were greatly afraid

That they reached
The gates of death

And Noah prayed
Unto the Lord
And cried unto him

On account of this

And he said
"O Lord help us
For we have no strength

To bear this evil
That has encompassed us

For the waves of the waters
Have surrounded us

Mischievous torrents
Have terrified us

The snares of death
Have come before us

Answer us O'Lord
Answer us

Light up the countenance
Toward us
And be gracious to us

Redeem us
And deliver us"

And the Lord hearkened
To the voice of Noah
And the Lord remembered him

And a wind passed
Over the Earth
And the waters were still

And the Ark rested

The Ark rested

★★★

Can you keep a secret?

The Kurdish old man

Asks the boy

A 300 year old secret

Ali Kaderi Sunay

Uncle of the boy's mother

Can you keep a secret?

A 300 year old secret

About a cave

In the Valley of the Spirits

A cave

High up on the mountain

God's mountain

Can you keep a secret?

Promise me

No one from the outside

May know

What I am about to tell you

No one may know

It's all for us

Me

Ali Kaderi

Kept secret
For 70 years

And now I am telling you

You have a glow
About you

A glow about you

There was an earthquake

And volcanic eruption

1870

And the structure
Was moved

No one
Has found it since

No one has found it

But maybe one day

You will Dev

You will Dev

★★★

We read the Nordic Sagas
For possible clues

Possible clues

The Sagas believed

To be real history

Not fiction

According to
Icelandic Sagas

Erik the Red's Saga

Saga of the Greenlands

Plus chapters
Of the Houksbok

And the Flatey Book

The Norse started
To explore lands

West of Greenland

Vikings

Only a few years
After the Greenland settlement

985 AD

Old Norse word Saga
Is cognate to English ""say"

Meaning in Old Norse

"What is Said"

Tale

Story

Narrative

Originally transmitted
Orally

Very words
And deeds of the ancestors

9th to 11th centuries

2 centuries
Before being written down

They went on board
And sailed out to sea

Once more

Once more

They found
A second country

And again
Dropped anchor

Put out a boat

Went ashore

Level and wooded

With broad white beaches

Wherever they went

And a gently sloping
Shoreline

Leif said:

"I shall give this
Country a name

That fits with its
Natural character

And call it Markland"

The Land of the Forests

Ernie uses
World View 3 satellite sensor

Eyes in the Sky

We're going to find us
Some Vikings Sam!

They can't hide from us

Or I'm not
The Space Archeologist!

Multi-payload
Super spectral
High resolution

Commercial satellite sensor

Operating at altitude
Of 400 miles

Bingo Sam!

Bingo!

Point Rosee

Newfoundland

Straight lines indicate

Remnants of structure

Remnants of structure

Alter the surrounding soil

Changing amount
Of moisture

Affects the vegetation
Growing directly over it

Variations in plant growth

Form spectral outline
Of what was there

Centuries earlier

Satellite images
Taken in the Fall

Grasses in the area
Particularly high

Easier to see
Which plants

Are healthier

Drinking more water
From the soil

The place screams
Excavate me Sam!

Excavate me!

The Space Archeologist
Strikes again

Could be Ernie
Could be

Imagine the grants
We'll get Sam?

Imagine!

The commissions we'll get Sam!

Ka-ching!

A second Viking site
In North America!

We're gonna win the war Sam!

I hope you're right Ernie

In one area

Magnetometer survey
Reveals a hot spot

Partially surrounded
By straight lines

Indicate possible ruins
Of a small structure

We read the Nordic Sagas
For possible clues

Possible clues

The Sagas believed

To be real history

Not fiction

Nobody would have
Ever found L'Anse aux Meadows

If it weren't
For the Sagas

L'Anse aux Meadows

Jellyfish Cove

Northernmost tip
Island of Newfoundland

Discovered
In 1960

Only Viking settlement
Ever found in North America

Until possibly now

Possibly now

Ka-ching Sam!

Ka-ching!

Seven excavations

1961 to 1968

Until sufficient evidence
To confirm

It was Norse outpost

A bronze pin

A needle bone

A stone lamp

Most Norse possessions
Don't preserve well

Typically made from wood
Which decays

Or Iron
Which can decay too

Or gets melted down
To make something else

Eyes in the Sky

Eyes in the sky

Excavate me!

The Space Archeologist
Strikes again

Do I hear documentary Sam?

About us?

Commercial satellite sensor

Operating at altitude
Of 400 miles

World View 3

Eyes in the Sky

Magnetometer readings

Of remote side

Place called Point Rosee

Grassy headland

Above rocky beach

An hour's trek
From the nearest road

Elevated iron readings

We head off
To Newfoundland

It screams excavate me Sam!

Excavate me!

A dark stain

With buried
Rectilinear features

Optimum site
For Norse settlers

A dark stain

Southern coastline
Of the peninsula

Relatively few
Submerged rocks

Allows for anchoring

Or even beaching ships

Broad vantage point
To spot potential hostiles

Climate soil
Well suited for growing crops

Ample fishing

Game animals inland

This is our Goldilocks Sam!

Just right

Just right

Lots of natural resources

Such as chert
For making stone tools

And turf for
Building house

And most valuable
Resource of all

Bog iron

Type of ore
That forms

When rivers
Carry dissolved particles

Of iron
Down from mountains

Into wetlands

Oxidation may occur

Through enzyme catalysis

By iron bacteria

Just right

Just right

Who's your daddy?

Their very way of life
Depends on iron

Metal nails
Hold their ships together

7000 nails

From 880 pounds of iron

Which means that blacksmith

Had to heat and process

70 tons of raw iron ore

Eyes in the Sky

Eyes in the sky

It screams excavate me Sam!

Excavate me!

The Space Archeologist
Strikes again!

Excavation reveals

Remains of what appears
To be turf walls

And an iron working hearth

Bingo!

Nailed i!

Could be Ernie

Could be

To untrained eye

The hearth doesn't
Look like much

A boulder
In front of a shallow pit

Surrounded by
Smaller stones

But traces
Of charcoal

And 25 pounds
Of slag in the pit

Suggests that hearth
Used for roasting ore

First step in working process

Before metal cold be melted
And forged by a blacksmith

The ore needed
To be dried out

Otherwise would explode
When placed inside a furnace

Explode

Roasting process
Also removed

Some of the impurities
In the form of discarded metal slag

Ernie:
Big guy
Gray hair in a pony tail

Camouflage outfit

There were fuckin Vikings here Sam!

Do you know what this means?

Do you know what this means?

Southernmost
And westernmost

Known iron working site
In pre-Columbian North America

Turf structure
That partially surrounds the hearth

Nothing like shelters
Built by indigenous peoples

Who lived in Newfoundland
At the time

Nor by Basque fishermen
And whalers

Who arrived
In 16th century

Ernie smiles

Eyes light up

Fuckin Vikings Sam!
Has to be

Who else was mining
And roasting bog ore?

Jackpot Sam!

Jackpot

We won the war Sam!

We have to get radiocarbon tests Ernie

Of course we do Sam

But who the hell else
Could it be?

We have to make sure

Of absence of
Historical objects

Pointing to any other cultures

Any other cultures

Ernie takes a piece of ore

And I don't tell him

But so do I

I don't know why

His tests come back

Bingo Sam!

Bingo!

The Space Archeologist
Strike again!

Ka-ching!

They found that
It was a lovely wooded country

And that the woods
Ran almost down

To the sea

With a white,
Sandy beach

The sea was full
Of islands

And great shallows

Nowhere did they find
Any vestiges

Of men or animals

Except a wooden granary
On the islands

To the west

They sailed along
The coast to the east

Into some nearby
Fjord mouths

And headed for
A jutting cape

That rose high
Out of the sea

And was covered
With woods

And anchored the ship
And laid down a gang plank

"This is beautiful
And here I should like
To build me a home

A home"

★★★

Here we are
In the Valley of the Eight

The Valley of the Eight

When they find out
We are here

For Nuhun Gemesi

Nuhn Gemesi

Noah's Ark

They point to
Mt. Ararat

13 miles away

Which rises
Into the mist

Rises into the mist

And at the end of seven days
In the six hundredth year

Of the life of Noah

The waters of the Flood
Were upon the Earth

And all the fountains
Of the deep

Were broken up

And the windows of heaven
Were opened

And the rain was upon
The Earth forty days

And forty nights

Stones
Found on the hillsides

Of these valleys

Southwest of Mt. Ararat

How did they end up here?

So high

Rising into the heavens

Many of the stones
Have crosses on them

8 crosses

Byzantine
Armenian

That curve outward
At the top

Engraved after stones rediscovered

Probably by crusaders
Armenians

The name of the Village
Arzap or Arzep

Possibly comes
From the Turkish

"Arz zapt"

Which means
To capturethe Earth

Or possibly further back
From Semite

"In esetz tsap"

Can be translated

To cling to the Earth

Cling to the Earth

1960

Ron Wyatt

27 years old

Working as
A nurse anesthetist

In a hospital
Madison, Tennessee

Sees a photograph
In Life Magazine

Boat-shaped formation

Boat-shaped formation

At Durupina site
On a mountain

Near Mt. Ararat

Boat-shaped formation

Obsesses Ron

18 miles south
Of Mt. Ararat

The Lord is telling me
That it's Noah's Ark

Noah's Ark

From 1977
To his death in 1999

Makes over
130 trips to Middle East

Founds
Seventh Day Adventist Church

When he runs out of money overseas
He heads back home to his job

Earn more money
To fund his work for the Lord

Lives in simple duplex
Outside of Nashville, Tennessee

Filled with bookcases
Of archeological works

A woman is in the hospital
For delivery of her baby

Ron and she pray to the Lord
Before the procedure

The baby is born
Stillborn, lifeless

The woman screams
And cries

Looking around the room
For Ron

He is crouching
In the corner

Ron has a close relationship
With the Father

Goes to Him
To ask for his help

In this desperate moment

As Ron is praying
A bright light

Begins to shine
In the room

A bright light

The doctors and nurses
Recognize something unnatural

Is happening

A bright light
Engulfs the room

Something is
About to happen

The baby starts
To cry

Starts to cry

People say
That miracles follow Ron
Miracles

A humble servant
Of the Lord

Claims over the
Course of his life

To have found

The Ark of the Covenant

Only a High Priest
Went into the Most Holy Place

Once each year
To sprinkle blood

On the Ark of the Covenant

Sprinkle blood

So in our day

It is only Ron Wyatt
Who entered Most Holy Place

A cave

To take a sample
Of the blood of the Messiah

And have it analyzed
For the world to see the lab report

When the Ten Commandments
Come out of the cave

Along with video
Of him removing the Commandments

From the Ark

Never a second witness
That goes into the Most Holy Place

In the day of Moses

The people believe
The man that is proven to be

A man of the Lord

The Ark of the Covenant

Anchor stones
Or drogue stones

Used by Noah
On the Ark

Grave markers
For Noah and his wife

The Tower of Babel
In Southern Turkey

Site of the Israelite crossing
Of the Red Sea

Located in
Gulf of Aqaba

Chariot wheels
And other relics

Of Pharaoh's army
At the bottom

Of the Red Sea

Site of the biblical
Mt. Sinai

In Saudia Arabia
At Jabal al Lawz

Site of the crucifixion
Of Jesus

But people
Always skeptical

Scientists intrigued
And then they step back

Always think
Is another hoax

Where is the evidence?

There is nothing conclusive

Nothing conclusuve

Never stops him

He is doing
The work of the Lord

I am his servant

And nothing beats
His Ark obsession

Years of obsession

The Lord is telling me
That it's Noah's Ark

Noah's Ark

He and his two sons

Find themselves
At risk

In a strange country
Among people of strange speech

Attempt to rob
And kill them

A "nervousing experience"

Term coined
By youngest son Ronny

Beginning of many years
Of slow, meticulous

Frustrating research

That culminates
In what he claims

Is undeniable proof
Of the reality

And location
Of the remains

Of Noah's Ark

Noah's Ark

On their first try

A series of remarkable
And related discoveries

One after another

Several massive
Drogue stones

Bear eight crosses
Iconographic representation

Of the eight survivors
Of the Flood

Inscribed by
Byzantine and Crusader Christians

Proves that something
Or someone

Convinced them

That these pierced stones

Were relics from Noah's Ark

Noah's Ark

Find two grave markers

Bear the eight cross symbols
Of Noah and his family

A petroglyph
Portraying Noah's death

On one marker

That of his wife
On another

Petroglyph of a wave
With a ship atop it

Is to Ron
Obvious reference

To Ark and the Flood

Locate and photograph
Several other inscriptions

And physical remains
Of the Flood and the Ark

Get a brief look
At boat-shaped formation

Before they're forced
To flee for their lives

Arrive back
In Tennessee

Super eight movie film
Developed

Delighted to see
They have

Good photographic documentation
Of all the artifacts

And inscriptions

Informed about
A Dr. William Shea
M.D. ph.D

University of Michigan

Several articles
He has written

Believes boat-formation

At Durupina site

Could possibly
Be Noah's Ark

Excited

Contacts Dr. Shea

Shares their discoveries

The Lord has lead me to you

He is delighted

Reviews inscriptions

Recognizes pierced drogue stones

Probable relics

From the Ark

Joins Ron
In applying to Turkish government

Permission to excavate
Boat-shaped formation

Permission declined

Declined

Same reply
After second request

They're stymied

Ron and his sons
Spend the summer of 1978

Locating and documenting

Site where Moses
And Hebrew slaves

Crossed the Red Sea

But they can't
Get the Ark

Out of their minds

Ron
Salt and pepper beard

Highlander hat

The Lord is telling me
That it's Noah's Ark

Noah's Ark

Ron's family
And trusted friends

Pray that the Lord
Will send an earthquake

That in some manner
Will expose the boat formation

Without any injury
To any inhabitants

Expose the boat formation

But Noah found favor
In the sight

Of the Lord

These are the descendants
Of Noah

A righteous man

Blameless in his generation

Noah walked with God

Three sons

Shem
Ham
Japheth

Now the Earth
Was corrupt

In God's sight

And the Earth
Was filled with violence

"Now I am going
To destroy them

Along with the Earth

Build yourself an ark
Of cypress wood

Expose the boat formation

People say
That miracles follow Ron
Miracles

A humble servant
Of the Lord

Ron watches evening news

Thrilled to see
That an earthquake

Hits area
Where remains are located

No casualties

Thank you Father

Makes arrangements
To return to the site

Arrives early summer
1979

The formation
Has been split down the middle

Entire length

And the earth
Has fallen away

From all sides

Ron takes clean
Fresh samples

Carefully measures
Length of the object

Documents dimensions
Of main structural timber

That are exposed

Photographs it

Returns home
With lots of

Archeological data
And 3 specimens

Selects Gailbrath Laboratories
Knoxville, Tennessee

Because they're highly
Recommended

Entrusts the care
And analysis of these precious samples

To them

Results are astounding

Astounding

Raw carbon content
Shows object to be

Composed of
Decayed wood

High concentration
Of oxidized metal

Is shown

3 samples taken
From the site

At distances
That guarantee

Them to be out
Of the geological influence

Of the boat remains

Compares favorably
With chemical values

Of normal countryside

Proves that boat formation
Composed of decayed

And oxidized
Archeological remains

Shares data
With Dr. Shea

It's Noah's Ark!

Noah's Ark!

On the strength
Of the evidence

Reapplication to
Turkish authorities

Once again
Put off

I'm not giving up

They have to let us back

I am going to pray

Pray

And they do

And more stunning announcements

Revelations

But the naysayers
Weigh in

Weigh in

He planted the samples

He is a religious fanatic

A Creationist

There was never any ark

Hoax!

Weigh in

Apparently first seen
By Kurdish farmer

Following an earthquake
May, 1948

World's attention
Drawn to this

Streamlined boat-shape
By publication

Of aerial photograph
Taken by Turkish Air Force pilot

In Australian Pix Magazine
July 9, 1960

And American Life Magazine
September, 1960

Another earthquake
December, 1978

Said to have
Enhanced the relief

Between boat-shaped formation
And surrounding terrain

But the particular
Boat-shape

Is far from unique
In this landscape

Far from unique

The Turkish Air Force
Release photo

Showing three
Smaller boat shapes

In the mud flow
Of the foot slopes

Nearby lesser
Mt. Ararat

If not for the fact
That this particular boat-shape

Is apparent length
Of Biblical Noah's Ark

Then little attention
Would be paid

It is much wider
Than the Ark

Though proponents
Of the site

Sat that is because
Outside walls splayed out

By weight of mud

Site properly known
As Durupia

Named after
Turkish army captain

Who first saw
The boat-shape

On the aerial photograph

And involved
In first expedition
1960

Counts 80,000 stories

In 72 languages
About the Flood

70,000 include a boat

In 1951
Spends 12 days

40 companions

To no purpose
Ice cap of Ararat

"Although we found
No trace of Noah's Ark"

Declares later

"My confidence
In the Biblical description

Of the Flood

Is no whit less

We shall go back

We shall go back"

Noah walked with God

Encouraged by Dr. Smith

Young Greenland explorer

Jean de Riquer

Climbs volcanic peak
In 1952

Comes back with nothing

Comes back with nothing

My confidence
In the Biblical description

Of the Flood

Is no whit less

No whit less

80,000 stories

In 72 languages
About the Flood

70,000 include a boat

We shall go back

How did they end up here

So high

Rising into the heavens

Little village
In Turkey

Now called Arzep

Also called

Sagliksuyu

Or Sa Lik Suxu

Acid water in Turkish

Stories of the Flood

Found throughout the world

Old legends
And myths

Most include narrative
Of people being saved

In a boat

Strange if these stories
Come out of pure imagination

Independent of each other

2000 to 3000 years old

Accounts full of
Local differentiation

But the essence
Is the same

The essence
Is the same

All point to idea

There really was at one time
In history of mankind

A great flood

Is no whit less

Site endlessly promoted
By self-styled Archeologist
And explorer

Ron Wyatt

Repeatedly tries
To interest other people

In the site

Claims he has petrified wood

But the source is unclear

Former astronaut and Ark hunter
James Irwin

ICR scientist
John Morris

Neither of these men
Convinced after on-site inspection

Neither of them convinced

Former merchant marine officer
David Fasold

And geophysicist
Dr. John Baumgardner

Have parted company
With Wyatt

After cautious optimism

Even Dr. William Shea
 walks away

Using standard
Beach combing type metal detector

Type with
Disc shaped detector head
On the end

Of a long pole

"Hot spots"
Were indeed found

But randomly
Distributed

Not in regular pattern

Along lines

That Wyatt claims

Alleged
That metal detector survey

Using a molecular frequency
Generator/Discriminator

Mapped out
Those "iron lines"

Which represent
Longitudinal cross beams

Containing iron nails
And/or brackets

But, again, results
Of this technique

Considered untrustworthy

Untrustworthy

Brass welding rods
Being used

In essence
As divining rods

Similar to the use
Of a forked stick

To search
For water

Iron lines
On diagram

Of the boat-shape
And the lines of plastic tape
In photographs

Are only interpretation
Based on results

From pseudo-scientific instrument

Both Dr. Baumgardner
And Dr. William Shea

Are in Turkey
July, 1986

Waiting for Wyatt
To join them

At the site
Without a permit

And in 30 minutes

Make 10 passes

With radar scanner

Only over the southernmost
Portion of the boat-shape

The so-called "prow"

Results inconclusive

Inconclusive

Upon meeting Wyatt

Provides them with copies
Of his own scans

Legitimizes claim
By invoking name

Of Tom Fenner
Geophysical Survey System, Inc.

In New Hampshire

Who looked at scans
And informed him

Formation
Is man-made boat

Show series
Of laterally
Periodic narrow reflections

Stacked in
Column-like structures

At approximately
The same depth

Roughly equidistant

Give "non-natural"
Impression

At first glance

However
Interpretation of radar scans

Does not take
Into account

Crucial topographic
Surface variations

Across the site

Geophysicist Tom Fenner:

"I was surprised
And dismayed

That Mr. Wyatt
Was using my name

As well as
Geophysical Survey Systems, Inc.

In order
To lend credibility

To his unsubstantiated claim

Concerning the so-called
Noah's Ark site

Neither I
Nor GSSI

Believe the formation
To be man made"

Many claimed
To have found it

A shadow
That could be Noah's Ark

But Noah found favor
In the sight

Of the Lord

These are the descendants
Of Noah

A righteous man

Blameless in his generation

Noah walked with God

Three sons

Shem
Ham
Japheth

Now the Earth
Was corrupt

In God's sight

And the Earth
Was filled with violence

"Now I am going
To destroy them

Along with the Earth

Build yourself an ark
Of cypress wood

The waters of the Flood
Were upon the Earth

And all the fountains
Of the deep

Were broken up

And the windows of heaven
Were opened

Statements
From many travelers

Over the ages

Quoting people
Who say

"It is up there
On Mount Ararat"

Sometimes

A black spot

On one of the sides
Of the mountain

Is pointed out

Said to be the Ark

Knowledge of the position
Of the Ark

Gradually disappears

Disappears

After volcanic eruption

During time of Jesus

Or centuries after

Blasting one side of the mountain

Devastates whole area

★★★

And a wind
Passed over the Earth

And the waters
Were still

And the Ark rested

And the fountains of the deep
And the windows of heaven

Were stopped

And the waters decreased
In those days

And the Ark rested
Upon the mountain
Of Ararat

Rested upon the mountain
Of Ararat

And the Lord hearkened
To the voice of Noah

And said to him

"When thou shall have completed
A full year
Thou shall go forth"

And at the revolution
Of the year

When a full year
Was completed

Of Noah's dwelling
In the Ark

The waters were dried
Off the Earth

And Noah put off
The covering of the Ark

And the day came
That the Lord told them

To go out
And they all went from the Ark

The sons of Japeth
Spread towards the west
And got Europe

Sham's descendants
Got what later became
The Arabic lands

And Ham's descendants
Got Egypt and Africa

Here we are
In the Valley of the Eight

When they find out
We are here

For Nuhun Gemisi

Nuhun Gemisi

They point to
Mt. Ararat

13 miles away

Which rises
Into the mist

Rises into the mist

News from Turkey

Ernie had snuck off

And found the secret site

Found the secret site

Or so he claimed

Dev deeply insulted

Hired Murat Camping

Competitor of his

Took him to crevasse
Which held some room

Deep down

That looks like the footage
Claire sent me

Ernie ranting
To the media

Ranting

Film scene

Built by Dev
From old planks

From Trabzon
On the Black Sea

Allegation
Based upon statement

From anonymous local person
Who is said

To have taken part
In building the film scenery

In video and photos

Ernie is showing
A board

Said to have
Been found floating

At the bottom
Of a crevasse

Blackened by soot
Or ashes to make it

Look old

But when sown through
Appears to be

Light on the inside
And evidently

Not old

Not old

Dev is outraged

But makes odd statements

Won't reveal
How he found the cave

Or where it is

Says Ernie
Did not go to the real site

Trying to discredit him

Ruin him

Dr. Ernest Beard
Renowned archeologist

Nicknamed
The Space Archeologist

Uses satellite imagery
To find important archeological sites

Numerous Egyptian antiquities

The alleged second Viking site
In North America

Is not
From Noah's Ark

But from
A more recent date

Accuses Dev
Of cheating the Chinese

AIR Ministries

Ark is Real Ministries

Perpetuating
Known hoax

Frantic text from Claire

He's gone crazy Daddy!

Ernie's gone crazy!

He's trying to destroy us

I don't know why

Why would he do this?

Why?

Dr. Claire Richardson

Releases press statement

Infuriated by
Dr. Beard's baseless claims

Not even sure
If he is a proper scientist

Not sure
Of his credibility

Stand behind
Their find

And in time
The truth will win out

The truth will win out

Convinced
That the find

Is genuine

With regards
To board

Shown by Beard

That board
Must have been planted
By Beard and others

To throw suspicion
On our find

When looking
At the surroundings

In Beard's pictures

"I can see
That it is somewhere else

Other than where
We have been"

Ernie fires back

Fires back

Releases letter
From two Turkish brothers

Davut and Erkan Advar

Claim to have taken part

In building the wooden structure

Up on the mountain

For Derim Akar

Otherwise known as Dev

Letter so incriminating

Chinese have to deviate
From the plan

Of waiting patiently

Now even friends
Begin to question their find

He's destroying us Daddy

Destroying us

It's not even the site

Claire tracks
Down brothers

Only ones
In the neighborhood

With these names

Video put
On the internet

Brothers maintain
That they never

Wrote said letter

Content of letter
Isn't true

Show their passports

Write their signatures

Clearly shows
That signatures in letter

Have been forged

Forged

AIR threatens
Legal action

Against Ernie

Ernie fires back

Never sent
Carbon 14 test stating

That it was
4800 years

This test
Strongest evidence

That it was
Ark that they found

And yet

They don't release it

Hide the location

They don't release it

They're hoaxers

Hoaxers

Dr. John Boswell
Archeologist

Harvard University

Head of
The Paleontological Research Corp

Provide comprehensive analysis
Worldwide

Archeological remains

Complete comparative examination

The site is remarkable

Remarkable

States Boswell

Comprises

A large all-wood structure
With an archeological assemblage

Appears to be
Mostly from late Epipaleolithic Period

Radio carbon dates
From between 13,100 – 9,600 BC

Wonderfully preserved
Exhibits wide array

Of plant materials
Including structures

Made of cypress

One room with a floor
Covered by chickpea seeds

Most impressed
By artifact assemblage

Particularly basalt bowls
Stone cores
And debitage

Based upon objects at site
Suggests that

Dates back
To an earlier period

More than the 4800 BC
That radiocarbon dating

Of the Chinese
Allegedly shows

But other finds
Are of more recent date

Two small ceramic bowls
From Chaleolithic Age
(5800 – 3000 BC)

And Bronze Age
(3000-1200 BC)

Placed in one of the rooms
Of the structure

If it is the Ark

Earlier objects
Could have been brought

Before the Flood

And the newer ones
After the Flood

Surface scatter

Of wood above
Large structure

121 meters in length
23.8 meters wide

Construction at least
5.2 meters deep

Several measurements
Of exterior walls

Exhibit angles
Moving inward

Through base
Of edifice

There are
Stair-like features

Descend through middle
Of multi-storied structure

Mortise-and- tendon construction

Large wooden structure
Located on Mt. Ararat

With what appears to be
Mostly Epipaleolithic assemblage

Is noteworthy

Is no hoax

The Chinese
Dated it wrong

Team comprised of people
With limited archeological experience

Instead of obtaining samples
From cores

And unexposed locales

And wrapping them
In tin-foil

Surface samples
Were retrieved with bare hands

Or cotton gloves

Date most likely
Reflects a sample

That was contaminated
By ancient visitors

Or modern explorers

Most of the assemblage
Portrays a much earlier period

Much earlier period

Is remarkable

Remarkable

So one can see
Its magnificent peak

From far away

Mighty and beautiful

Attracts visitors

Frightens the locals

Know how dangerous
It is

Caught in sudden snowstorm

Fall into a glacier

Walk around it

50 miles

All of the stories

How dangerous

Impossible to climb

The Holy Mountain

Doomsday Mountain

Also called the Maternal Mountain

The Mountain of Pain

But Noah found favor
In the sight

Of the Lord

These are the descendants

Of Noah

A righteous man

Blameless in his generation

Noah walked with God

Now the Earth
Was corrupt

In God's sight

And the Earth
Was filled with violence

The whole Earth
Flooded for about a year

Even highest mountains
Covered with water

I text Ernie

What are you doing Ernie?

What have you done?

Why?

Why?

A call from Jack

He's breathing heavily

Are you ok?

Everything all right?

I'm ok

But one of us is missing

It's fucked up

Tucker is missing

Tucker?

What happened?

It was last night

We were around a campfire

He was drunk
And stoned

And got really crazy

Incoherent

Falling over

Got into an argument

With this guy Ted

Ted pushed him

And he wandered off

When he didn't come back

We tried to find him

We tried to find him

But we couldn't

So we called the cops this morning

They're looking for him now

I hope they find him

Jack and I

Watching
The mother osprey

Flying around

Hovering

2 feet in length

6 foot wingspan

Soar high
Above their prey

Then dive feet first
Full force

Dive

Into the water

Fully submerged

Brings up its catch

Brings up its catch

Feet have barbed pads

Evolved to help them

Hold slippery fish

Carry the fish head first

For aerodynamic flight

Thunders off

Thunders

★★★

We read the Nordic Sagas
For possible clues

Possible clues

The Sagas believed

To be real history

Not fiction

According to
Icelandic Sagas

Erik the Red's Saga

Saga of the Greenlands

Plus chapters
Of the Houksbok

And the Flatey Book

The Norse started
To explore lands

West of Greenland

Vikings

Only a few years
After the Greenland settlement

985 AD

Old Norse word Saga
Is cognate to English "say"

Meaning in Old Norse

"What is Said"

Tale

Story

Narrative

Originally transmitted
Orally

Very words
And deeds of the ancestors

9th to 11th centuries

2 centuries
Before being written down

They went on board
And sailed out to sea

Once more

Once more

They found
A second country

And again
Dropped anchor

Put out a boat

Went ashore

Level and wooded

With broad white beaches

Wherever they went

And a gently sloping
Shoreline

Leif said:

"I shall give this
Country a name

That fits with its
Natural character

And call it Markland"

The Land of the Forests

Ernie uses
World View 3 satellite sensor

Eyes in the Sky

Bingo Sam!

Bingo!

Point Rosee

Newfoundland

Straight lines indicate
Remains of structure

Alter the surrounding soil

Changing amount
Of moisture

Affects the vegetation
Growing directly over it

Variations in plant life

*The Space Archeologist
Strikes again*

Ka-ching!

A second Viking site
In North America!

We're gonna win the war Sam

Eyes in the Sky

Eyes in the sky

A boulder
In front of a shallow pit

Surrounded by
Smaller stones

But traces of charcoal

And 25 pounds
Of slag in the pit

Suggests that hearth
Used for roasting ore

There were fuckin Vikings here Sam!

And do you know what this means?

Do you know what this means?

We have to get radiocarbon tests Ernie

Of course we do Sam

But who the hell else
Could it be?

We have to make sure

Of absence of
Historical objects

Pointing to any other cultures

Any other cultures

Ernie takes a piece of ore

And I don't tell him

But so do I

I don't know why

His tests come back

Bingo Sam!

Bingo!

*The Space Archeologist
Strikes again*

Ka-ching!

A few weeks later

I get my test results back

When I see the results

I get it tested again

And again

And again

I call Ernie

We have a problem Ernie

What do you mean?

I took a sample too

You what?

Why didn't you tell me?

I had it tested 4 times

It's not Norse

It's only 400 to 500 years old

What lab did you use?

Beta

Well they're wrong!

They're wrong!

They're not wrong Ernie
They're one of the best labs

You know that

This is not good Sam

We have to think about this

Let's think it through

Let's not do anything rash

Promise me that Sam

In spite of this
They put to sea

As soon as they
Could get ready

And sailed for 3 days

There was no land
In sight

The fair wind
Died down

And they were
Beset by fogs

And north winds

Until they lost all
Track of their course

This went on
For many days

And then the sun
Came out again

So they could
Get their bearings

They hoisted sail
And sailed all day

Before they sighted land

They wandered what country
This might be

It could not be Greenland

It could not be Greenland

★★★

Call from Claire

Any news from Jack?

I tried to call him
Did they find Tucker?

I told him not to go gorge diving

People get killed

Tucker is missing Claire
It's not the diving

Hundreds of people
Are searching

State Police

Going to join the search myself

Long red hair

Thin
5 feet
11 inches tall

Was last seen
Wearing black Slayer tee shirt

Ripped blue jeans

We are praying for Tucker
Here in Turkey

Praying for him

A few hours later

His body is found

His body is found

In an inlet

Off Taughannock Falls

100 foot gorge

He probably just fell in

Didn't see it

On whatever he was on

Makes the local news
Big deal around here

Big deal

On any given summer day
Thrill seekers

Flock to the area

Jump from
Several heights

Into the 12 to 15 feet
Of water

100 foot gorge

Are you okay Jack?

Yeah, I'm okay

Just really sad

I wish I could have done more

I wish I could have saved him

Nine campers

One of them accidentally
Fell his death

Tucker Caldwell
18 years old

Of East Ithaca

One time co-captain
Championship Little Red soccer team

His body
Found in an inlet

2 pm

There were nine campers

One of them accidentally
Fell to his death

Claire calls

And she calls Jack

He had his problems Jack

But he's with the Lord now

May the God of hope
Fill you with all joy and peace
As you trust in him

So that you may overflow
With hope
And the power of the Holy Spirit

A few months later
AIR
Ark Is Real Ministries

Fund raise
For a new project

Ark Park

One to be opened
Outside of Hong Kong

The other to be opened
At as site near Memphis, Tennessee

Ark Park

Go to Graceland

And then the Lord's Park

Will feature
Full size replica Noah's Ark

Built according
To dimensions in Bible

Spanning 510 feet long
85 feet wide

51 feet high

A modern engineering marvel

Seven stories tall

Football field and a half long

Largest timber frame
Structure in the world

How big was Noah's Ark?

How did Noah
Fit all of those animals aboard?

How did he feed
And care for the animals?

How did Noah
Build the Ark?

We're building
The Full size Noah's Ark

To answer these questions

How long is a cubit?

A cubit an ancient measurement
Of length

Based on the distance
From the elbow

To the fingertips

At Ark Park

You'll learn how long
3000 cubit really is

300 cubits in length
50 cubits in width
30 cubits in height

Ark Park

Can you keep a secret?

A 300 year old secret

About a cave

In the Valley of the Spirits

A cave

High up on the mountain

God's mountain

Can you keep a secret?

Promise me

No one from the outside

May know

What I am about to tell you

No one may know

It's all for us

It's all for us

Ernie uses
World View 3 satellite sensor

Eyes in the Sky

Eyes in the Sky

Pointed at Turkey

Specifically Mt. Ararat

Come on baby
You can't hide from me

Or I ain't
The Space Archeologist

You can't hide from me

No sirree

No sirree

You can't hide from me

Bingo!

Bingo!

The Space Archeologist
Strikes again!

Here we are
In the Valley of the Eight

The Valley of the Eight

When they find out
We are here

For Nuhun Gemisi

Nuhun Gemesi

Noah's Ark

They point to
Mt. Ararat

13 miles way

Which rises
Into the mist

Rises into the mist

And at the end of seven days
In the six hundredth year

Of the life of Noah

The waters of the Flood
Were upon the Earth

And all the fountains
Of the deep

Were broken up

And the windows of heaven
Were opened

And the rain was upon
The Earth forty days

And forty nights

The windows of heaven
Were opened

Here we are
In the Valley of the Eight

Noah and Naameh
His 3 sons
And their wives

The Valley of the Eight

When they find out
We are here

For Nuhun Gemisi

Nuhn Gemisi

They point to
Mt. Ararat

Which rises
Into the mist

Rises into the mist

And the windows of heaven
Were opened

Little village
In Turkey

Now called Arzep

Also called

Sagliksuyu
Or Sa Lik Suxu

Acid water in Turkish

We are shown
These strange large stones

Huge headstones
That look like anchors

Have been found

They have
Or had

Holes on top

Some are still intact
Still see the holes

Here in this village
And throughout hills

Surrounding the region

Thirteen such stones
Have been found

Thirteen such stones

2 even 3 meters

Holes in the stones
Are special

Slope inwards

Fit to tie a rope

So knot
Slides into the hole

Stays put

Create a drag
In the water

If attached
To the end of a boat

Drag produced
As wind driven boat

Pulls it along
The roughest water

Will cause
Boat's hyper dynamic

Pointed bow or stern
To face into the wind

The oncoming
Wind-blown water

And the windows of heaven
Were opened

And the rain was upon
The Earth forty days

And forty nights

The windows of heaven
Were opened

When they find out
We are here

For Nuhun Gemisi

Nuhun Gemisi

Without such a device
A wave can hit the boat

Turn it sideways
To the wind and waves

Next wind impacting
The side of the boat

Will have a greater
Likelihood of rolling boat over

Sea anchors
Drogue stones

Prevent this

Might anchors of stone
1500 meters above sea level

Mighty anchors of stone

Here we are
In the Valley of the Eight

The Valley of the Eight

Stones
Found on the hillsides

Of these valleys

Southwest of Mt. Ararat

How did they end up here?

So high

Rising into the heavens

Many of the stones
Have crosses on them

8 crosses

Byzantine
Armenian

That curve outwards
At the top

Engraved after stones rediscovered

Probably by crusaders
Armenians

The name of the village
Arzap or Arzep

Possibly comes
From the Turkish

"Arz zapt"

Which means
To capture the Earth

Or possibly further back
From Semite

"In esetz tsap"

Can be translated

To cling to the Earth

Cling to the Earth

They point to
Mt. Ararat

13 miles away

Which rises
Into the mist

Into the mist

Stones in front
Of very old stone house

In a flat open field

Engraved on one of them

A rainbow
Over eight people
A rainbow

Half of them
Have long hair

Half of them
Long beards

6 of them
Are smaller

Then the other two

Noah and Naameh

She is looking down

Eyes closed

Maybe she died first

Both have closed eyes

Bowed heads

Another stone

A boat on top of a wave

Quite a sight

So high up here
In the mountains

No lakes or seas

A boat on top of a wave

How did they get here?

How did these stones get here?

They're huge

No one knows Jack

They're beautiful

Here we are
In the Valley of the Eight

The Valley of the Eight

When on the seventh day
He set forth a dove

And released it

No perch was visible
So it came back to him

He set forth a swallow
And released it

No perch was visible
So it circled back to him

He set forth the raven

And released it

Beat its wings

Flew off

It never came back

It never came back

www.ingramcontent.com/pod-product-compliance
Lightning Source LLC
Chambersburg PA
CBHW030824090426
42737CB00009B/862